HEART to HEART

A Daily Devotional for Teenage Girls

REBECCA LYN PHILLIPS

OLIVER
NELSON

THOMAS NELSON PUBLISHERS
Nashville

For Mommy
You have a golden heart.

Published in Nashville, Tennessee, by Thomas Nelson, Inc., Publishers, and distributed in Canada by Word Communications, Ltd., Richmond, British Columbia.

Unless otherwise noted, the Bible version used in this publication is THE NEW KING JAMES VERSION. Copyright © 1979, 1980, 1982, Thomas Nelson, Inc., Publishers. Scripture quotations noted CEV are from the Contemporary English Version. Copyright © 1991, American Bible Society. Scripture quotations noted NIV are taken from the HOLY BIBLE, NEW INTERNATIONAL VERSION ®. Copyright © 1973, 1978, 1984 by International Bible Society. Used by permission of Zondervan Publishing House. All rights reserved.

Some names and events have been fictionalized to protect privacy.

Printed in the United States of America.

Library of Congress Cataloging-in-Publication Data

Phillips, Rebecca Lyn, 1975–
    Heart to heart / Rebecca Lyn Phillips.
       p.   cm.
    ISBN 0-8407-9219-0 (pbk.)
    1. Teenage girls — Prayer-books and devotions — English.   I. Title.
BV4551.2.P48   1994
242′.633 — dc20   93-39054
                                                                    CIP

1 2 3 4 5 6 — 99 98 97 96 95 94

Contents

Acknowledgments

I am grateful for the help of Bill Watkins, who instilled in me the tenacity to learn and refine. I am also thankful for Victor Oliver's confidence in my ability, Rose Marie Sroufe's encouragement and concern, Brian Hampton's editing skill, and the kindness of all the others on the Oliver-Nelson team.

– 1 –

God's Creation

The heavens declare the glory of God;
And the firmament shows His handiwork.

Psalm 19:1

The sun shone brightly as I walked onto the beach. It was a perfect day to relax on the warm sand. Watching several children squeal with excitement as they rushed into the splashing waves, I remembered how jubilant I was the first time I saw the huge ocean.

Feeling content and renewed already, I placed myself in the sand at the edge of the blue ocean water. The foam from the crashing waves splashed onto my legs and hands. I watched the waves silently form and then tumble with a loud crash. The sounds filled my ears and slowly drew my mind into the motion of rising and falling. I could hear nothing else.

Lord, what peace is found in listening to the sounds of Your world! The sights and sounds take me into Your presence and display Your beauty. I lose awareness of myself and become enclosed by Your light.

I usually take the beauty of the earth for granted. I get too distracted to be still and gaze at its loveliness. I don't stop long enough to hear its gentle sounds.

All creation communicates something about You. The mountains tell of Your steadfastness; the birds demonstrate Your gentleness; the flowers display Your flawless beauty; and the ocean shows the depth of Your love.

I need to get out of the house and enjoy Your creation

more because I then experience You more deeply. I need to feel the earth's revitalizing power.

Thanks for the magnificent way You speak to me through nature. Now I know You even better.

Next time you're outside, look around and listen to the peaceful sounds of nature. What message is God communicating to you?

REFLECTIONS: _____

_____

_____

_____

_____

_____

_____

_____

_____

_____

_____

_____

_____

_____

_____

− 2 −

Seeds

I planted the seeds, Apollos watered them, but God made them sprout and grow.

1 Corinthians 3:6 CEV

I never thought anyone would notice the Scriptures I had taped in my locker until the boy two lockers down asked about them. A few days ago he walked over to me.

"What is that in your locker?"

"Bible verses," I replied.

He looked puzzled. "Why do you have them?"

"To encourage myself."

"Oh . . . neat," he responded simply.

No more was said between us. Maybe I should have done more explaining, but hopefully I'll have another opportunity to talk to him about You. At least a little seed was planted. A thought was placed in his mind, producing curiosity. Is this what You mean by being a witness?

I never believed small examples of Christianity could add up to much. I'm the kind of person who hopes for on-the-spot conversion: I share, they hear, they believe. It's like instant oatmeal—quick and easy. I should consider a more creative approach, for You use people in many different ways to tell the awesome message of Your salvation. I don't have to present this message in a way that makes both me and the listener uncomfortable.

I need to understand the power of planting seeds in new and fresh ways. I need to realize that my smile, the Scriptures in my locker, the love I demonstrate to the unpopular people at school, the respectful way I talk to my teachers, and the words I say to those around me make an impact. They are like all kinds of seeds that You can use to bring the people of the world to Yourself.

Help my life exhibit Your magnificent love. Bring opportunities that I can use to influence others and share Your power to give life that lasts forever. Show me the effectiveness of planting seeds that can spring up unto eternal life.

Do you have a hard time sharing Jesus with those around you? Ask God to show you new and creative ways of sharing — of planting seeds.

REFLECTIONS: _____

_____

_____

_____

_____

_____

_____

_____

_____

_____

_____

True Success

But he who is greatest among you shall be your servant. And whoever exalts himself will be humbled, and he who humbles himself will be exalted.

Matthew 23:11–12

I watched the Grammy Awards last night. The singers and songwriters looked classy in their expensive evening gowns and tuxedos. The performers sang with confidence and style.

I became more and more jealous as I watched singer after singer receive a Grammy. I longed to be one of them, waltzing up to the stage to receive my award. How I wish I could be recognized by millions of people. To receive sackloads of fan mail, to appear on national TV and magazine covers — it all sounds like the ultimate thrill!

I wonder if receiving a Grammy provides neverending happiness and excitement. Does the ecstasy of that golden night last a lifetime? I wonder if appearing on TV and posing on magazine covers creates a continual fulfillment.

I have received awards for my accomplishments. Friends have envied me, and adults have applauded my achievements. How proud I am when I'm honored before my peers!

Father, being recognized for outstanding achievements is good and estimable. And, of course, everyone loves to be exalted, no matter how long the excitement lasts. Rewards not only generate confidence but encourage determination to be the best one can be. However, they don't provide true happiness, do they?

What does provide true satisfaction and happiness, dear God? I'm afraid it's not posing on magazine covers and singing love songs.

Is a humble servant what You deem praiseworthy? Does being a servant produce true joy? Oh, how difficult it is to be Your servant! Living to genuinely love others and serve them requires a strong character—definitely different from the world's view of stardom.

Help me to be a servant, Father. Help me to see that servanthood will give me joy and unfathomable rewards from You—rewards that last forever!

Ask God to show you how fulfilling it is to be a servant. Ask Him to show you how to be a servant.

REFLECTIONS: _____

_____

_____

_____

_____

_____

_____

_____

_____

Living in the "Real World"

The LORD will perfect that which concerns me;
Your mercy, O LORD, endures forever;
Do not forsake the works of Your hands.

Psalm 138:8

Will high school ever end? I feel depressed. At times the days pass so slowly. I get up, go to school, come home, do my homework, get up, go to school, come home, do my homework. Life is boring. I wish something exciting would happen to brighten up these long days.

I can't wait until I graduate! Then life will be exciting, but frightening. What will I do? I have several ideas about what I'd like to do after high school, but none of them really stand out as "the thing to do." Graduation seems far away and yet close.

Father, will I like being on my own? Now that I think about it, it sounds scary. Cooking for myself, having to take care of my own car, buying my own necessities, and looking out for myself will be challenging. I won't be able to run to Mom when I am sad or frightened or ask Dad for help with my homework. I will have to depend totally on You to take care of me.

Will I like the "real world"? Is it unfeeling and uncaring, as adults say it is? What will my career be? Sometimes I think I'd love to move to the inner city to help the poor and outcast. Yet when I jog away from my neighborhood, I get scared and feel insecure. I think, "If I feel like this now, what will happen when I'm really out on the streets, helping the poor?" I get tired of being around my family, going to high school, and living in this familiar neighborhood. But when I think about how big and over-whelming the "real world" is, being with the people I know and love feels good.

Father, will You please help me to enjoy this time at home and not despise it? Will You please be my constant, ever-present Friend when I leave home? I will try to trust You in all things so that no worry about the "real world" will fill my mind. Thank You for the potential to be on my own, but thanks for this stage of my life too. Please help me to make each day of my life fulfilling.

Do you ever get scared thinking about the future and living in the "real world"? Tell your Father in heaven why you are scared. He will comfort you.

REFLECTIONS: _____

_____

_____

_____

_____

_____

_____

_____

_____

Understanding God's Grace

And He said to me, "My grace is sufficient for you, for My strength is made perfect in weakness."

2 Corinthians 12:9

I can't believe I didn't finish my history homework last night. My teacher asked for it today and in front of the class I had to say, "Uh . . . I didn't get it done." I was so embarrassed I cried, which made me look even more stupid.

It's humiliating to mess up like that. I wonder what people think of me when I blow it. I know what I think of myself when I do. I tell myself I'm a failure who can't do anything right. I feel embarrassed and ashamed — like I've let You down.

I see my life as a multitude of performances at which I fail or succeed. Instead of laughing at the times I fail, I think about them for a long time and replay what the situation would have looked like if I hadn't messed up. It's hard for me to move on without remembering past mistakes and sins. I can't seem to forgive myself and forget them.

I confess my sins to You, but I don't feel different. I plead repeatedly, "I'm so sorry. Please forgive me," as if You can't understand me and need to be told again and again.

People tell me I'm too hard on myself. I need to depend on Your grace, but I don't understand Your grace. Is it like a blanket that hides my sin? What is its function? How can it help fix my problems?

Please help me understand what grace is and how it fits into my life. I want to quit feeling bad about myself. Please give me insight into this concept and help me apply it to my life in a dynamic way.

Do you get confused about what grace is and how it fits into your life every minute of the day? Someone has said grace is "God's Riches At Christ's Expense." Verses that discuss grace are Romans 5:17–20; 6:14; 2 Corinthians 9:8; Galatians 2:21; Hebrews 4:16.

REFLECTIONS: _____

_____

_____

_____

_____

_____

_____

_____

_____

_____

_____

_____

_____

Alone and Afraid

For I am persuaded that neither death nor life, nor angels nor principalities nor powers, nor things present nor things to come, nor height nor depth, nor any other created thing, shall be able to separate us from the love of God which is in Christ Jesus our Lord.

Romans 8:38–39

I'm new in my youth group. I don't know anyone. I feel uneasy when I go to Sunday school because they laugh and talk to their little groups of friends without noticing me. I feel out of place—like I don't belong. I sit alone and watch what seems like a circus. I wish I felt bold enough to take part in the fun.

It would be nice if someone would come over and talk to me. Maybe they don't know what to say, or maybe they don't even care. Still, I'd love for someone to notice me and at least say "hi."

It's hard to be new. I don't know anybody, and to get to know someone I have to risk being thought of as "nerdy" or "weird." Part of me says to jump in and be myself, but the other part says I'd better not try it because they might not like the "real me."

I want to be liked, God. I want others to think of me as a neat person. How do I get them to see me that way?

If I take a risk and introduce myself to those in the youth group, will You give me confidence? I'll be myself if I know You'll be there to encourage and support me.

Please help me release my fears. I want to get to know

these people and be their friend, but it's scary. I need Your help and Your boldness to feel comfortable in meeting them and showing them what kind of person I am. Help me to be confident in who I am so I can feel good about myself as I talk to them.

Try to remember when you were new to a group or school. Did you ask God to help you overcome your apprehension?

REFLECTIONS: _____

_____

_____

_____

_____

_____

_____

_____

_____

_____

_____

_____

_____

_____

Annoyed to Death

A soft answer turns away wrath,
But a harsh word stirs up anger.

Proverbs 15:1

As I was trying to get my homework done tonight, my sister kept coming in my room, laughing and running around like a hyena. I asked her to leave and she replied, "But I love to bug you!" I threatened to inflict bodily damage, but she continued her escapade, undaunted. She jumped on my bed and sang in such a loud voice I had to scream to get her attention. "I'm trying to do my homework, Loudmouth, so leave my room and quit being such a pain!" Thankfully my mom intervened and got rid of the pest before I completely lost my cool.

She seems to be on a "bug my sister" crusade. She starts going wild, and I feel like I can't escape. I keep trying to convince my mom to send her to the zoo. She'd fit in and enjoy being among her own kind.

I love my sister. We have fun together. Ninety-nine percent of the time we get along great, but when she is in a wild mood and I'm not, my patience wears thin. She bugs me at the wrong times—while I'm studying, reading a novel, or listening to my favorite CD. I think she enjoys agitating me; she loves to see me jump up and yell at the top of my lungs. I don't start out that way, but she pushes me even after I've gently and politely asked her to stop two or three times.

Give me patience with my sister so I won't scream and

cause an uproar. I need to be mature enough to talk to my mom and dad about the problem instead of creating more of one by getting upset. I complain about her wildness; but when I yell, I'm acting as crazy as she is. Please help me to have more patience and to control my temper. I want our relationship to be a good one, even though we have problems.

Does someone in your family annoy you? How do you handle the situations in which he or she bugs you? How do you think God wants you to handle them?

REFLECTIONS: _____

_____

_____

_____

_____

_____

_____

_____

_____

_____

_____

Mornings

My voice You shall hear in the morning, O LORD;
In the morning I will direct it to You,
And I will look up.

Psalm 5:3

I want to go back to bed. I don't want to face the morning. My mind tells me I must begin my day, but my body shouts, "I need sleep! I need sleep!" Just as I'm about to give in, my alarm clock goes off. It will always be my worst enemy.

I slowly stagger into the bathroom as if in a trance. Looking in the mirror, I realize why I need more sleep. "I shouldn't have gone to bed so late," I tell myself.

When I make it to the breakfast table, my sleepiness has changed to grouchiness. I don't even try to muster enough energy to speak to my family except to gripe at my sister, who is loudly slurping her cereal.

That's how my mornings begin, Father. When I think of all I have to do, I become overwhelmed. I want to hide in my cozy bed, where I can escape.

Must every morning be the same? I dread each one. I don't know how I could be one of those people who shoots out of bed like a rocket, with a smile already plastered on his face. I'm one of those who needs to wear a sign saying, "Just woke up. Stay away."

I try to be enthusiastic in the morning, but I fail. I'm always grouchy and sluggish. I excuse myself by saying that I'm not a "morning person," but nobody in my family buys it.

Please give me a big boost in the mornings. I need help badly. I need to anticipate each day with enthusiasm, but that seems impossible. Please make it possible, God. If I look forward to each new day, I'll be more energetic and less lazy. Please help me see every day as a chance to live triumphantly.

Do you dread getting up in the morning? If so, how can you change that outlook?

REFLECTIONS: _____

_____

_____

_____

_____

_____

_____

_____

_____

_____

_____

_____

_____

Supermom

She opens her mouth with wisdom,
And on her tongue is the law of kindness.
She watches over the ways of her household,
And does not eat the bread of idleness.
Her children rise up and call her blessed;
Her husband also, and he praises her.

Proverbs 31:26–28

My mom is one of the wisest people I know. She gives me advice that, as far as I can remember, has always worked. She looks at life from such a different perspective that I often wonder if You've given her an extra dose of insight.

I usually get so emotional about my problems that it takes me hours to think of solutions, but my mom gives practical solutions so quickly that I wonder if she even had to think about it. When I'm faced with a situation that could turn out good or bad, she reminds me to "think positive until proven otherwise." I get upset about situations like that and other problems I face, but she analyzes the circumstance, determines the solution, and doesn't worry. I consider that impossible!

When I went on a school trip a few weeks ago to Texas, she advised me to take a jacket, umbrella, and my old tennis shoes in case of rain. "But it's not the rainy season," I argued and ignored her advice. When we got to Texas, it rained the entire week.

My mom has an astounding intuition. When we were

eating supper a couple of nights ago, no one was talking. Suddenly she said to my dad, "Honey, you need to stop worrying about Patty Shultz. It will work out." My dad had not even mentioned his problem with Mrs. Shultz, yet my mom knew exactly what was on his mind.

My mother is an amazing woman. She is wise, perceptive, compassionate, and has an unusually positive outlook on life. When I need help, I know exactly who to turn to.

Thank You for blessing me with a strong and caring mother. She is always there for me when I need her. She loves her family passionately and serves us with humility and grace. I couldn't have asked for a better mom. Move over, Superman, 'cause here's Supermom!

God has blessed many mothers with special gifts. What are the qualities you admire most in your mom or someone who is like a mom to you?

REFLECTIONS: _____

_____

_____

_____

_____

_____

_____

_____

– 10 –

Sex

Do not be deceived, my beloved brethren. Every good gift and every perfect gift is from above, and comes down from the Father of lights, with whom there is no variation or shadow of turning.

James 1:16–17

You have given us many gifts to show that You are a God of love and power, and sex is one of them. Many people take this gift and abuse it. They make light of its meaningfulness on TV, in the theater, and at school. They exploit Your gift of sex. They make it into what they want it to be. In one movie I saw, a couple was in bed. The man said, "Hey, honey, let's just have sex one more time. Then you can go home to your husband." They proceeded, took quick showers, and went their separate ways, feeling empty and unsatisfied.

No! No! I don't want to listen to the world tell me to go ahead and have sex when I feel like it. Yet, oh God, at times I do want to listen to this message. When I do, my passion blinds me, and I long to have sex before I get married. Then I feel horrendously guilty, like someone who flings herself to the winds of passion. And so my attitude toward Your gift of sex is dirtied in my mind—until I tell You I've sinned by dreaming of what it would be like to have sex before marriage.

But, Father, although You do restore the way I think of sex when I make this confession, another problem arises. Some Christians have messed up my view of sex by talking about it as if it is something bad. So, Father, how can I have a balanced view? How am I supposed to look forward to having sex when I get married if I either feel wretchedly guilty or passionately aroused when the thought of sex crosses my mind?

Oh God, I want to be healthy sexually because my sexuality definitely is a part of me and will always be. So please help me to see sex as You want me to see it. Eliminate this passion and guilt from my heart. Don't let me be infected by what the world shows Your gift of sex to be. Show me its loveliness, its innocence, and its place. Tell my heart that it is good.

Do you sometimes feel lustful and then guilty when you think about sex? If you do, how do you think this attitude can be changed? What is a healthy attitude toward sex?

REFLECTIONS: _____

_____

_____

_____

_____

_____

_____

_____

Painful Love

*A new commandment I give to you, that you love one another;
as I have loved you, that you also love one another. By this all
will know that you are My disciples, if you have love for one
another.*

John 13:34–35

I listened attentively to the song playing on the radio.
The words were touching. The singer sang about how
hard it is to love someone after that person has hurt you
over and over. As she sang I thought of a parallel in my
own life. I have been struggling with hate and resentment
toward someone close to me—someone who has hurt me
repeatedly.

Each day I grow more bitter. I think to myself, "How
unfairly you've treated me!" Every time I see this person
I cringe and list the wrongs done me. I often recite in my
head the dark words, "I hate you! I hate you!" I feel like
two people—one who loves and is happy and one who is
hurt and spiteful. The two don't mix well. Yet I don't
know how to rid my heart of this hate because it is strong
and seems rational. Because of the way my life has been
messed up by my "enemy," I sometimes make myself believe that hatred is acceptable and understandable.

How can I possibly have the energy to love that person
again? Where can I find the strength? I do not want to be
hurt any more. God, I am afraid to love.

Please show me how to be loving. Most important, give
me the power to decide to love, for that is the most diffi-

cult and crucial part. When I am tempted to give in to bitterness, help me to say, "Satan, I resist you in the Name of Jesus Christ. I will not give in to hatred." Please help me to be an instrument of love and forgiveness even when doing so is painful.

Choosing to turn from hate to love is hard when someone has hurt you. Learning to love that person again sometimes takes a long time. However, once the decision is made, the struggle against resentment weakens and the power to love becomes greater. Do you need to choose to love?

REFLECTIONS: _____

_____

_____

_____

_____

_____

_____

_____

_____

_____

_____

_____

Without Fear

Peace I leave with you, My peace I give to you; not as the world gives do I give to you. Let not your heart be troubled, neither let it be afraid.

John 14:27

There have been three robberies in my neighborhood in the last two weeks. A neighbor told me that the two guys who broke in were armed. Four times yesterday when my dad answered the phone, the caller immediately hung up. Many of our neighbors have had the same thing happen to them. Perhaps the robbers are calling to see if we're home.

I have always thought of my neighborhood as a haven, a place free of crime. My mom and I used to go on walks and leave the door unlocked. Every day I see reports about murders, kidnappings, rapes, robberies, or drug busts; but I never thought I'd have to worry about something like that happening to me.

I shouldn't be scared, but I am. I'm frightened not only about the robbers, but also about the loonies and drunks who walk the streets at night and the gangs in our city. I've already encountered too many men who have looked at me in the wrong way. They didn't appear to have good intentions.

The world isn't a safe place anymore. It doesn't take long to discover its dark side.

Help me balance protecting myself in practical ways and trusting You. It's hard not to get carried away with installing alarm systems and dead bolts, carrying around Mace everywhere I go, and keeping the shades shut all the time so no one can see in the house.

Please help me live in such a way that I am not bound and caged by my fear. Remind me to pray every day for protection for my family so fear will not gain a hold on me. I need to protect myself, but I also need to remember that You are my ultimate protection. Thoughts of Your power can bring me peace.

Have you had an encounter with crime? Think of some practical ways to protect yourself, and remember that God is always watching over you.

REFLECTIONS: _____

_____

_____

_____

_____

_____

_____

_____

_____

_____

_____

– 13 –

Hard Decisions

The Lord answered, "Martha, Martha! You are worried and upset about so many things, but only one thing is necessary. Mary has chosen what is best, and it will not be taken away from her."

Luke 10:41–42 CEV

When my mom and I went shopping last week, I saw a desk I loved instantly. I've been needing a new one because mine doesn't have enough drawers. I hadn't seen any that I liked, though. When I saw this desk, I thought, "This is the one." Then I looked at the price tag. "It had better be 'the one' if I'm going to pay that much," I figured.

My mom and I talked about the pros and cons of buying it. She said I wouldn't be able to go to camp with my youth group if I bought the desk because I had promised to pay for the cost of camp. I argued, "But, Mom, you know how badly I need a new desk. Can't we split the camp cost?" She said no, that I had to decide what I wanted more—to go with my friends and have a time of relaxation and spiritual renewal or to buy a desk that I both needed and liked. That night I stayed up late trying to make a choice I knew I wouldn't regret. I thought of the good and bad consequences of each decision and tried to figure out which one I could live with more easily.

I decided to buy the desk. It was the only one the store had, and I'm glad I got it when I did. I missed going to camp with my friends, but I can go next summer. I had fun working at my new desk at home. I made some preparations for the start of school that I couldn't have done if I had gone to camp.

I'm glad I took the time to decide the best way to use my money. I work hard for it and don't want to regret the way I spend it.

Please help me take the time to discern how to use my money wisely, even when I want to buy something right away. Keep me from making impulsive money decisions so that I will be pleased with the choices I make.

Do you use your money without considering the drawbacks? How can you be sure the decisions you make will be the best?

REFLECTIONS: _____

_____

_____

_____

_____

_____

_____

_____

_____

_____

_____

Talents

Each of you has been blessed with one of God's many wonderful gifts to be used in the service of others. So use your gift well.

1 Peter 4:10 CEV

I got my ACT scores back today. I was disappointed with my math score, but fairly pleased with the others. As I was comparing scores with my friends, Christy walked up and asked me how I did. I reluctantly told her, knowing she had probably received a much higher score. When she told me hers, my mouth dropped. I felt stupid for having shared my score because hers was nearly perfect!

Since then I've been thinking about the great chance Christy has of being accepted to a prestigious university. How can she be that smart? I don't feel pleased with my scores any more.

It's hard to be glad about other people's accomplishments. I want to be the best in everything I do; I can't rest in the knowledge that there are people who are better in some areas.

I must remind myself that You have given me unique gifts and talents—talents I can use in unique ways. It helps to think of famous people like Mother Teresa. She may not be good at playing basketball; but when it comes to serving the poor, she's the best. She has learned to use her talent to the maximum.

Help me to develop and use my talents to my best ability. Then, when others succeed, I can be happy for them, knowing that I am a success too.

What are your talents? Are you developing and using them to the highest degree?

REFLECTIONS: _____

_____

_____

_____

_____

_____

_____

_____

_____

_____

_____

_____

_____

_____

_____

Purity

Do you not know that your body is the temple of the Holy Spirit who is in you, whom you have from God, and you are not your own? For you were bought at a price; therefore glorify God in your body and in your spirit, which are God's.

1 Corinthians 6:19–20

During Sunday school, one of the girls in my youth group announced in a quivering voice that she is pregnant. Suddenly, everyone became silent; we were shocked. We know the statistics of teenage pregnancies, but now it was happening to someone we know.

She continued to explain that the sex education classes ensure that if you take precautions, you won't get pregnant. "I did what they said, but it still happened," she lamented. She said she was happy but frightened. "I'm only eighteen and I'm not ready for this. All my plans must change."

As tears of confusion and despair dropped from her pretty eyes, my heart was quiet with reflection, pondering what I would do if I became pregnant before marriage and feeling relieved that I wasn't. I am grieved because of her situation, but am glad for its warning.

Father, I know that safe sex doesn't consist of wearing condoms and taking birth control pills. The only safety is in waiting until marriage. However, many people argue that teens can't help it—that we need an outlet for our raging hormones. "You can always take preventive measures" is their contention. The truth is that often they aren't enough. Painful STDs can be contracted, and many times pregnancies do result. And no one says anything about the guilt, shame, and agony teenagers endure after having premarital sex.

For a teenager, to abstain from sex is one of the most difficult things in the world. Our hormones run wild, and self-control seems like an impossible virtue. When I'm on a date with my boyfriend, trying to make my head control my emotions is like trying to keep a traveler from gulping water after walking through a desert for ten days without it.

You knew what You were doing when You commanded purity. You knew the devastation that results from having sex before marriage. You knew that waiting would be best for us because of what it prevents and because of the joy and satisfaction it produces.

Father, help me to use wisdom when I am dating so I will not be carried away by my passion. Show me how to find a balance between my head and my heart. Teach me that waiting will bring great pleasure and fulfillment and glory to Your Awesome Name.

Ask God to help you develop ways of keeping yourself pure.

REFLECTIONS: _____

_____

_____

_____

_____

_____

_____

– 16 –

Endless Worry

Look at the birds in the sky! They don't plant or harvest. They don't even store grain in barns. Yet your Father in heaven takes care of them. Aren't you worth more than birds? Can worry make you live longer?

Matthew 6:26–27 CEV

I worry too much. I've been worrying so much this week that I've had to force myself to eat. I'm afraid that someday I'll shrivel up and blow away.

Even when things are fine, I'm anxious. Never able to clear my mind, I always think of something to fret about. I worry about school, chores, my room, family fights, planning for college, clothes, money, a job, our dog barking at the neighbors, my nails . . . No matter how unimportant and trivial something seems, it can fill my mind for an entire day or even a week. I can hardly get to sleep at night because there's always something bugging me. I try to reason with myself, telling myself that worrying doesn't help, but it's no use.

My mind seems to be filled with a million sticky notes flying around. Written on each one is something to worry about. No matter how hard I try, I can never get rid of them all. As soon as I take care of one, another note appears. It's a pattern that never stops.

I want everything to be perfect and all to go smoothly, but that desire will never come true on earth. Somehow I think that if I take care of everything, I'll be calm and happy. I can't believe I've tricked myself into thinking I can accomplish that task! No wonder I'm never calm and at peace!

Father, I need Your help. I've tried to rid my mind of worry again and again, but I've failed. Please rescue me from this pattern that robs me of the joy in life. Help my mind to rest.

Do you worry a lot? How can you overcome anxiety's grip on your mind?

REFLECTIONS: _____

_____

_____

_____

_____

_____

_____

_____

_____

_____

_____

_____

_____

When Guys Don't Make Sense

Those who are wise will shine like the brightness of the heavens . . .

Daniel 12:3 NIV

When I was in the eighth grade I had a crush on Jacob Riley, the most popular guy in school. He was the best player on the football team and a straight-A student. My friends and I dreamed of what it would be like to be his girlfriend. Any girl with brains would have considered it a dream come true to catch the attention of Jacob.

At a party some of my friends and I had a chance to talk to him. I had a fantastic time, and I admit that I flirted like crazy with him. Remembering the time now, I laugh at how in love I was and how silly I acted. When it was happening, though, I saw my behavior only as having fun. Jacob laughed and seemed to be having fun too. I thought, "Hey! Maybe he likes me!"

The next week at school he smiled broadly when I passed him in the hall. We always said hi, and my excitement escalated as each day passed. Feeling daring, I wrote my phone number on a piece of paper and mailed it to him at the end of the week.

For three long weeks I waited for a call from Jacob. I was anxious and decided to reveal to one of my closest friends what I had done. She asked, "Don't you know he's going with that new girl?" I was shocked and horrified. I had been sure he liked me!

Recovering from my humiliation and disappointment took several weeks. I had been so confused that I felt incapable of showing interest in any guy.

I sometimes try to analyze guys' behavior, and once I've reached a conclusion about what it means, they disprove it. I wish we could be direct with each other. Trying to understand what each other is thinking usually ends in uncertainty.

Please help me avoid creating wrong assumptions about what guys are thinking. I don't want to jump to conclusions that would embarrass me. Help me learn how to communicate with them and not fabricate something that isn't there. I need to learn how to be wise in all my relationships.

Do you wish for a better understanding of the opposite sex? We need to ask God for wisdom in relating to guys.

REFLECTIONS: _____

_____

_____

_____

_____

_____

_____

_____

What's Most Important

And He said to them, "Take heed and beware of covetousness, for one's life does not consist in the abundance of the things he possesses."

Luke 12:15

As I rang Scott's doorbell, I was overwhelmed by the size of his house. It was more like a mansion. I compared it to my house. If his were placed next to mine, my house would seem the size of a garage.

Scott came to the door and welcomed me to the party. Not wanting him to see my amazement at his house, I acted like I didn't notice its enormity.

The inside was more overwhelming than the outside. My living room could have easily fit in the entryway. The stairs looked like something you'd see in a fancy home decorating magazine. There was even a large balcony.

After the party, my mom picked me up in our station wagon. Everyone at the party was standing outside when she drove up, and I felt like pretending she wasn't my mom. "How humiliating!" I muttered to myself as I waved good-bye to my friends.

As we drove off, I asked my mom why in the world she had to bring the old station wagon. Then I exclaimed, "Can you believe the size of that house? It's huge! I felt so stupid and out of place when I went inside."

My mom said she understood my feelings. She told me a story about a time she felt the same way. Then she talked about what's most important. She said that nice houses and cars and clothes don't make a person great in Your eyes; they don't define a person's worth. She said the way You value me doesn't depend on whether my family owns a Mercedes convertible or a Ford station wagon. What concerns You is the way I live my life.

Please show me how to live confidently, being sure of my value in Your eyes. Help me not to feel inferior to those who have more money than I do. Show me what is important to You.

Do you feel inferior when you're around people who have more money than you do? Are you inferior?

REFLECTIONS: _____

_____

_____

_____

_____

_____

_____

_____

_____

_____

_____

_____

Being Jesus to the Poor

For the poor will never cease from the land; therefore I command you, saying, "You shall open your hand wide to your brother, to your poor and your needy, in your land."

Deuteronomy 15:11

My mom and I drove to our city's rescue mission a few days ago to drop off some of my outgrown clothes. It's in the worst section of the city. As we went inside, we saw a woman with a tattoo and a short leather skirt, kids running around without shoes, and men using more bad words than I hear in a day at school. My mom and I felt out of place and uncomfortable among people who lead completely different life-styles than we do.

I don't see homeless people in my neighborhood, and I rarely see them at school or church. They are like a separate community with whom I seldom come in contact. When I see a homeless man, I feel pity toward him for a moment; but then I pass on without giving it further thought. Sometimes I feel guilty for not doing more than giving my old clothes. I tell myself that I should give all I can because they have nothing.

I should be willing to sacrifice time and money to help people who have nothing. Homelessness is a gigantic problem in America and around the world. Even though I can't see its widespread effect, I know it is a real-life issue that deserves more than our awareness. Homelessness needs to be fought with an energetic love and a courageous eagerness to "be Jesus" to the poorest and most oppressed.

Create in me a heart that desires to serve You by serving the homeless. Make it a longing and a passion so that I won't think twice about humbling myself to help them in whatever way I can. Make my eyes brave, not afraid to look at a homeless person and show my love—a love that doesn't take into account how bad the person smells or how dirty he or she looks.

Help me to "be Jesus" to the homeless. I want to have Your caring eyes, warm smile, and outstretched arms. I want to love them because You have chosen to love me.

Because the homeless situation is treated only as a social problem by the government, it is hard to see it as a spiritual issue that can and should involve Christians. How can you participate? How can you "be Jesus" to the poor and the hopeless?

REFLECTIONS: _____

_____

_____

_____

_____

_____

_____

_____

_____

Communicating with Parents

Children, obey your parents in all things, for this is well pleasing to the Lord. Fathers, do not provoke your children, lest they become discouraged.

Colossians 3:20–21

I just had an argument with my dad. I am so mad! He always assumes that I am telling him what to do—that I am challenging his authority. Today I asked politely if he could turn the TV off while I studied for a big test.

He replied, "No. Are you trying to tell me what to do? I don't think you understand. I am the father; you are the kid. You don't tell me whether I can watch TV or not."

Father, all I did was ask if he would mind turning the TV off while I studied for a test! Why was he so defensive? Why did he get so upset at such an innocent request?

I feel like my dad is on a completely different wavelength. It is difficult to communicate with him. We practically need a translator to explain to each other what we "really mean."

Arguing with either of my parents is never fun. I want them to value my ideals and feelings, for they are a part of me. I need them to listen to me.

God, I know that I am supposed to speak to my mom and dad with respect and humility. When I do, the situation is better, not only for me, but for the entire family. It is hard, though! I can't do it alone. I need You to create these qualities in me. And please help my parents to listen to me.

Many times it's hard to communicate with our parents. What can you do to improve your communication with your parents?

REFLECTIONS: _____

_____

_____

_____

_____

_____

_____

_____

_____

_____

_____

_____

_____

_____

Flawless Bodies

But the LORD said to Samuel, "Do not look at his appearance or at his physical stature, because I have refused him. For the LORD does not see as man sees; for man looks at the outward appearance, but the LORD looks at the heart."

1 Samuel 16:7

I wish I could change my body. Every day I think, "If only I didn't have so many freckles, such thin hair, or such big thighs." Rarely am I satisfied with what I see in the mirror.

Today I was looking at a magazine, and I gazed longingly at the pretty models with impeccable, shining complexions and perfectly sized legs. I'd look at a picture and then examine my own body in the mirror. As I compared mine to theirs, I groaned in despair. "God, why in the world do I have to look like *this*?" I pleaded.

The girls in those pictures seem to have what practically every girl would want—the adoration of handsome guys, the envy of other teenage girls, attention, admiration, wealth, confidence, and happiness. Their lives seem so glamorous, all because they're beautiful! If only I were as stunning as them. I could have my picture taken without agonizing over my nose appearing to be ten feet longer than it really is. I could go to school confident that I was looking good. I could have the attention of gorgeous guys.

Is this a fantasy, Father? Does beauty really guarantee happiness? I know an extremely attractive girl who wanted to kill herself. Boys drooled when they saw her walking down the hall, and almost everyone wanted to be her friend. Despite all that, she was truly miserable.

I need to remember that I possess qualities that beautify my inner self, qualities that many gorgeous girls lack.

Please help me to cultivate these qualities—my gifts and talents—and not to frustrate myself by wishing I had "the perfect body." Show me how to find my worth and happiness in knowing that though people look at the outside, You look at the heart.

Do you wish you had a flawless body? How do you think you can find peace with your body and with your whole self?

REFLECTIONS: _____

_____

_____

_____

_____

_____

_____

_____

_____

_____

The Gift of God's Spirit

If you then, being evil, know how to give good gifts to your children, how much more will your heavenly Father give the Holy Spirit to those who ask Him!

Luke 11:13

When I got up this morning and looked out my window, I saw a fresh, white blanket of snow covering the ground. It was our first snowfall of the year, and its pristine beauty filled me with a sense of awe. I eagerly took in its loveliness because I knew as soon as the children of my neighborhood woke to see the great white playground, the loveliness would be gone. In its place would be footprints and sled marks and patches of grass leading to funny looking snowmen.

In the same way Your Spirit is fresh. It's Your essence that falls on my soul like the first snowfall and gives me new peace and a feeling that life in You can be fun, like flying down a hill on a sled, or throwing snowballs at neighborhood friends, or flapping my arms and legs up and down to make an angel in the snow.

I can hardly describe this feeling I get from Your Holy Spirit: words don't seem adequate to express it. It's as if I'm at the foot of Your throne and You gently, quietly tell me to come to You and I do and You throw Your arms around me and hold me like I've never been held before and I'm overcome by Your love.

Oh, God! I lift my arms to You in praise, longing to see

You, to hear Your voice, and to hear You call my name. I sing and dance out of my joy and desire for You.

Sometimes, though, it's hard to feel Your Spirit's presence. I get down on myself; or I fill my heart with rage toward someone; or I become envious; or I depend too much on TV, food, music, or clothes to provide a pick-me-up. These attitudes and actions block Your Spirit from giving me true joy and peace and from cultivating in me love, faithfulness, gentleness, patience, kindness, goodness, and self-control.

Please keep me from getting wrapped up in sin and from trying to fill empty and hurting spots with things that don't help in the long run. Only Your Holy Spirit can give me the joy and peace I long for and the healing my heart so often needs.

Please fill me with Your Spirit today so I can get in touch with You in a powerful way. I thank You and praise You for giving us this life changing gift.

How can you feel the power of the Holy Spirit more deeply in your life?

REFLECTIONS: _____

_____

_____

_____

_____

_____

_____

Chores

Even a child is known by his deeds,
Whether what he does is pure and right.

Proverbs 20:11

Helping around the house is not on my list of the "Top Ten Most Fun Things to Do." I doubt it ever will be. I've almost considered saving my money to hire a cleaning lady so I won't have to scrub the toilet and other such joys.

There is always something my mom and dad want me to do. When I wake up in the morning, I know I'll be bugged with "It's about time to mow the yard" or "There's a load of towels needing to be folded." When I complain their response is, "We do a lot for you, and you can find the time to help us in some small way." I moan and groan, they get aggravated, and the chores remain undone.

My mom reads books and magazine articles about helping your child enjoy housework, but it's not changing anything. No one in my family has come up with a solution for the problem of chores, even though my mom tries by making charts and posters.

I know my attitude stinks. I realize I should obey with a cheerful heart. It's frustrating, though, because there's always something that needs to be done. I don't want to spend all my time cleaning.

How can I see this from a different perspective? I want to be able to see my chores as fun, but that seems like a joke. I just can't picture myself jumping up and down, screaming, "Oh, I can't wait! It'll be such fun!" when my mom tells me to wash the supper dishes.

Maybe I can make a compromise with my parents in which I promise to do my chores at a certain time every day if they will stop reminding me over and over to do them. Then we can be sure they'll get done, and they won't have to pester me about it.

Even if the compromise doesn't work, please give me the motivation to get my chores finished. I agree with You that I have been disrespectful and disobedient and need to do my chores whether I feel like it or not. Please give me the energy.

Do you think of housework as drudgery? What are some ways to make it less so?

REFLECTIONS: _____

_____

_____

_____

_____

_____

_____

_____

_____

24

God's Whispers

*Then He said, "Go out, and stand on the mountain before the
LORD." And behold, the LORD passed by, and a great and
strong wind tore into the mountains and broke the rocks in
pieces before the LORD, but the LORD was not in the wind; and
after the wind an earthquake, but the LORD was not in the
earthquake; and after the earthquake a fire, but the LORD was
not in the fire; and after the fire a still small voice.*

1 Kings 19:11–12

Today I saw one of the most beautiful rainbows I've
ever seen. It wasn't blurry or barely noticeable; each color
was distinct and brilliant. The arch seemed to spread
across the entire sky.

I don't see a rainbow very often. It's such an unusual
occurrence that when it happens, it's something special
and delightful to see — like a fireworks display. When a
rainbow appears I marvel at the timing because it always
encourages me when I seem to need help most.

I especially needed to be encouraged today because my
struggles have been making me feel like You aren't with
me. I've wanted You to speak to me in some way — to let
me know You care about me — but You've been silent.
Each struggle has seemed monstrous, and I've thought,
"Why doesn't God tell me what's going on? Why won't
He show me the reason for all these trials?" For a long
time I've needed a sign, assuring me of Your care and
faithfulness. Today You gave me one.

As I gazed at the rainbow, I knew You were saying to

me that You are always with me and that You know my struggles even when I don't feel like You care. You are a faithful God who promises to always take care of me.

I often want You to show me what's going on and why You are letting bad things happen to me. I expect a revelation or a wonderful feeling to well up inside. However, You don't choose to work that way all the time. Sometimes You speak in a whisper, as You did today through the rainbow.

Help me to be attentive to Your voice. Develop my ability to listen closely. Thank You for the way You speak to me. Even though You often speak in whispers, they are powerful and give me strength when I need it most.

Do you often feel that God is silent? Ask Him to teach you how to listen to His whispers.

REFLECTIONS: _____

_____

_____

_____

_____

_____

_____

_____

_____

25

Male Alert

*There is neither Jew nor Greek, there is neither slave nor free,
there is neither male nor female; for you are all one in Christ
Jesus.*

Galatians 3:28

The guys sitting next to me drooled at the model in the magazine. Several lewd comments were made about her body. As they laughed and made disgusting jokes, my anger boiled. How dare they view women as playthings whose only worth lies in providing sexual gratification! Can they not look beyond beautiful bodies to see the value of inner beauty?

It aggravates me to be around guys who apparently care for only one thing—bodies. To hear what they say makes me feel valueless and exposed. Even though the physical attraction of boys to girls deepens during teenage years, they shouldn't think of girls as toys. They should respect us as their equals spiritually and mentally and should treat us with dignity. No girl wants to be thought of as inferior or used as a doormat.

I have a friend whose boyfriend can't keep his hands off her. During class I see him rubbing his hand up her leg and hear him making comments to the other guys about the size of her breasts. She tries to scold him, but does so with a laugh, seemingly enjoying the attention.

That's not the kind of attention I want, Father. I desire a guy who values not only my body but my mind and spirituality as well. I want to have a relationship with someone who thinks of me as valuable and important.

Give me careful eyes that I may discern the "bad guys" from the "good guys." Don't allow me to be swayed by someone good-looking who only wants to use me. Please help me to save my love for the one who will treat me with dignity and gentleness.

Don't allow yourself to become involved with someone who treats you with disrespect. Ask God to protect you from these kinds of hurtful relationships.

REFLECTIONS: _____

_____

_____

_____

_____

_____

_____

_____

_____

_____

_____

_____

26

Healthy Anger

And the LORD uprooted them from their land in anger, in wrath, and in great indignation, and cast them into another land, as it is this day.

Deuteronomy 29:28

I have been curt with my mom all day. When she asked me if I had a good day at school, I coldly responded and quickly turned away. She reached out to hug me, but I would not let her. With my cold unresponsiveness, I knocked down each attempt she made to communicate with me. She asked me what was wrong, but I said nothing.

I am angry, God. I acted rudely toward my mom today because I was mad about last week's unresolved conflict. We had an argument and she expressed her anger, but I was not allowed to respectfully express how I felt. She wouldn't let me explain the reason I acted as I did.

I surprise myself by the length of time I can remain angry. My anger is like a weed that grows and, fertilized by frustration, eventually begins to wrap around the love in my heart, trying to squeeze the life out of it.

How unfair I have been to my mom! I have held on to my angry feelings and have not been honest with her. I should have explained the reason for my unresponsiveness when asked what was wrong, but instead I remained silent while allowing the anger to yell within.

Anger is potent and dangerous, easily able to be turned into bitterness. It is like a bomb that explodes whether held inside or turned out. It's also a natural emotion that is healthy when expressed in the right way.

Please show me how to release my anger in healthy ways. Help me to express it within the bounds of respect for others, especially my mom and dad. When I am asked what's wrong, please give me the wisdom to explain my feelings; and when suppressed, help me to remember to go to You for an outlet. Teach me what healthy anger is.

How do you express your anger? Would God mind hearing you express your indignation and rage to Him?

REFLECTIONS: _____

_____

_____

_____

_____

_____

_____

_____

_____

_____

_____

_____

_____

27

Insecurity

For God has not given us a spirit of fear, but of power and of love and of a sound mind.

2 Timothy 1:7

This week I am at a camp far from home with about three hundred other teenagers from across America. I feel so intimidated! I'm afraid of being rejected by these people. Some are loud and boisterous. When I am around them, I feel stupid and out of place.

I feel so insecure. When I talk to someone I am scared that I don't look pretty enough. I'm afraid that I appear shy and weak. I try to look as inconspicuous as I can. Sometimes I pretend that I'm looking for somebody when I'm really not, just so no one will know that I'm by myself.

I feel that there are many other girls with nicer clothes and prettier smiles. So many other teens have more outgoing personalities. I feel small and insignificant.

You're helping me, though, Father. You brought someone to me so that I can see I am not alone. I talked with a girl yesterday. She said she feels just as I do, even though I could not see why she feels insecure because she is so attractive on the outside. I said, "Wow! I think God knew I needed someone to talk to about this insecure feeling."

The feeling is still here, though. Father, I'm so afraid that my peers don't think I'm "good enough" for them. I feel that when I'm around them they look me over—size me up—and then either give their stamp of approval or the stamp that coldly says "reject." I can see it by their looks, or I think I can anyway. That is why I am so afraid to be myself and to introduce myself to all these other teenagers. I'm afraid my stamp will say reject, and then I will feel even worse about myself.

Father, please help me. Let me feel Your presence so that I will be confident. Help me to know that You love me no matter what I look like or whether I am loud and rowdy or quiet and shy. Help me to know in my heart that Your stamp is one of approval. Help me to know that when You size me up, even with all my flaws, You still love me and want me as Your special child.

Do you ever feel insecure around other people? How can you develop confidence in yourself, knowing that you are precious to God?

REFLECTIONS: _____

_____

_____

_____

_____

_____

_____

_____

_____

28

New Beginnings

Brethren, I do not count myself to have apprehended; but one thing I do, forgetting those things which are behind and reaching forward to those things which are ahead, I press toward the goal for the prize of the upward call of God in Christ Jesus.

Philippians 3:13–14

Today was a disaster. To start things off, I didn't get out of bed until ten minutes before time to leave for school. I was late to my first class and looked like a slob because I hadn't had time to take a shower. After lunch I got my physics test back, for which I had studied three hours, and was horrified to see a big, ugly *D* written in red. "All that work down the drain," I moaned. I had done my best and failed. I had wanted to go home and boast, "Mom, I got an *A* on one of the hardest tests I've ever taken." But now I had to break the news that I'd earned a dreaded *D*.

I thought nothing worse could happen until I went to track practice. I wasn't enthusiastic about running because I was upset about my physics test, but somehow I found the energy. As we were doing sprints, I twisted my ankle and fell with a thud. My mom came and drove me to the emergency room. To our relief, the doctor assured us that it was only a sprain.

I've been lying on my bed for the past three hours, wishing I could start this day again and make it different. It's one of the most disastrous days I've had in a long time—one of those about which you either laugh or burst into tears.

I'm glad only two and a half hours remain in this day. I want it behind me. At least I can begin again tomorrow. Tomorrow is a day with no mess-ups—not yet anyway.

Thank You for the chance to make new beginnings. It's nice to know whenever a day goes wrong that I can begin again.

Ask God to show you the power of new beginnings.

REFLECTIONS: _____

_____

_____

_____

_____

_____

_____

_____

_____

_____

_____

_____

_____

_____

29

Broken Families

He heals the brokenhearted
And binds up their wounds.

Psalm 147:3

My best friend confided to me that her parents are getting a divorce. I tried to console her, but my words of support seemed much too inadequate to soothe grief that deep.

She said she feels like her life has been torn apart. "How can I go on?" she implored as tears streamed down her cheeks. "My family is ruined."

I don't know if I could go on with life if my parents divorced. For my family to be split in half would be a nightmare. To have to witness the anger of my parents toward each other would be too much to bear. I know it would destroy part of my spirit because I have seen it happen to several of my close friends. One of them lived in a daze last year because of the turmoil at home. His parents fought constantly. His grades dropped from *A*s to *C*s and *D*s, his smiling face displayed a blank stare, and his connection with those around him became weak. It was as if his spirit of life was gradually disappearing.

Oh God, how damaging divorces are to the lives of the parents and children! No one is spared from the pain. It is not surprising that this world is filled with so many emotional scars and wounds. Divorce destroys, and only Your loving grace can heal the hurts that result.

Please wrap Your arms of love tightly around broken

families because they need Your love so much. Bring healing to emotional wounds. Have mercy on the sins of wives and husbands, and renew their souls as rain does a dry land.

Do you know someone whose parents recently divorced — perhaps your own? What steps can you take to bring healing to the situation?

REFLECTIONS: _____

_____

_____

_____

_____

_____

_____

_____

_____

_____

_____

_____

_____

30

Tongues on Fire

And the tongue is a fire, a world of iniquity. The tongue is so set among our members that it defiles the whole body, and sets on fire the course of nature; and it is set on fire by hell.

James 3:6

Katie's slumber party was off to a great start. We had gone to the grocery store and stocked up on munchies, rented our favorite movie, and bought a couple of magazines to catch up on the latest styles.

As we were getting settled for our evening of entertainment, the doorbell rang.

"I wonder who that is," I said.

Katie explained, "I forgot to tell you all that Kelly would be coming."

"Miss Bigmouth herself," I thought, trying to look excited.

Everyone welcomed Kelly to our night of fun. After saying "hi" to all of us, she dove right in. "You'll never believe who I just saw riding around with Matthew Gordon!" she exclaimed.

We were all ears.

"Cassy!" she divulged delightedly.

Cassy happens to be my best friend.

She continued, "Of course, we all know Cassy will do anything for a good time. I'm surprised she's not walking the streets downtown in that miniskirt she always wears."

Father, how could she say something so rude? If Cassy knew, she'd be crushed.

It's amazing how insensitive people can be. I've said cruel things behind other people's backs too, only to become aware of the hurt feelings I produced. Even though I apologized, I could never take back what I said.

Kelly's hurtful tongue has reminded me how destructive gossip can be. It can destroy friendships, mess up reputations, and ruin one's self-esteem.

I need to watch my own tongue by thinking before I speak, even though it's hard. Please help me. I want to speak words that uplift and encourage. I don't want to follow in Kelly's footsteps by saying things I'll regret. Please make my words pleasing.

Have you been hurt by gossip or been the object of gossip yourself? What does it produce?

REFLECTIONS: _____

_____

_____

_____

_____

_____

_____

_____

_____

_____

31

Complete Bliss

I charge you, O daughters of Jerusalem,
If you find my beloved,
That you tell him I am lovesick!

Song of Solomon 5:8

For almost two years my friend Tina has gone on and on about Patrick, a teenage guy who attends her church. She's told me that he's tall and handsome with beautiful eyes; that he plays basketball, baseball, and football; that he's on the honor roll and on the drama team at school; that he comes to church every Sunday even though his parents don't; and that he's one of the most sensitive guys she knows. Even after hearing all this, I never thought too much about Patrick. If he matched his description, I assumed he probably had girls after him all the time. I don't like to compete.

Then I saw him. I went to Tina's church one Sunday morning, and when I walked into the Sunday school room, my heart did gymnastics. I had never seen anyone that good-looking. I think my smile was the biggest in the history of smiles, and he gave a big smile back! Sunday school has never been as exhilarating as it was that day.

I've visited Tina's church several times since and have even gone out with the youth. He has been there every time, and I've been in heaven because I've caught him staring at me on several occasions. One time when we were talking, we gazed into each other's eyes for what seemed an eternity.

Being in love is thrilling. Daydreaming, wondering if he feels the way I do, not being able to eat because I'm lovestruck, smiling at every thought of his face, and analyzing his every move is fun and blissful.

Thanks for creating the attraction between guys and girls the way You did. It makes being a teenager exciting.

Isn't being in love an awesome experience? Our God delights in seeing us enjoy the gift of love He has given us.

REFLECTIONS: _____

_____

_____

_____

_____

_____

_____

_____

_____

_____

_____

_____

_____

32

Failure

The steps of a good man are ordered by the LORD,
And He delights in his way.
Though he fall, he shall not be utterly cast down;
For the LORD upholds him with His hand.

Psalm 37:23–24

I hate to fail. Yesterday I auditioned for a solo at school. I had practiced over and over. When the time came to try out, my heart was beating fast. I thought, "I can do this. I've practiced this song, and I know I can sing it with confidence."

The music began and I started to sing. My voice sounded as though someone were shaking me. I knew I was capable of doing a good job, but this time I blew it. I was devastated. I finished the song and, as I left, I punished myself with thoughts like, "How could you mess up so badly? How stupid!" There haven't been many occasions when I've been as angry at myself as I was then.

I didn't get the coveted solo, Father. Perhaps I could have if I had not been so nervous. Then I would be the one all the other girls would envy. I would be the one to receive the praise. I would be able to demonstrate my singing ability. Oh, why did I have to mess up?

Dear Father, I hate failure. It's embarrassing and humiliating—especially when I know I could have performed much better than I actually did.

Perhaps there are reasons for failure. I am sure of one reason: it humbles. I think I needed to be humbled because too many times I become arrogant and snobbish, thinking I am the best. I forget that You are the giver of talents and that it is by Your strength I succeed. Many times I believe I can achieve whatever I want on my own without You. Consciously I may not believe this statement, but it is still present in me.

Failure brings me to You so You can envelop me with Your comfort. You tell me that You don't expect perfection and that You love me even when I fail. You remind me that You are in control of all events in my life and that I must rest in that truth.

Please help me not to feel mad and humiliated about this experience. Instead, let me feel peace, knowing that I am not perfect. Help me to forget this failure and all other past failures so I can begin again.

Do you berate yourself when you fail? How do you think God feels about failure?

REFLECTIONS: _____

_____

_____

_____

_____

_____

_____

_____

_____

33

Priorities

Let your eyes look straight ahead,
And your eyelids look right before you.
Ponder the path of your feet,
And let all your ways be established.

Proverbs 4:25–26

A couple of nights ago when I was watching TV, my sister asked me if I would play a game with her. I was watching an episode I'd seen before and it wouldn't have killed me to turn it off, but instead I replied, "No, I'm watching TV."

Today I was reading a magazine and my mom asked if I'd enjoy going to get some ice cream—just the two of us—and I said I'd rather stay home. I don't know why I thought staying home to look at a magazine was more important than spending time with my mom. It was another of the bad decisions I've been making lately.

My priorities aren't arranged in the right order. I've been choosing TV and magazines over time with my family and haven't been spending enough time meditating on the Bible, talking to You, and helping others. You are of highest importance in my life, yet I've neglected our relationship as well as those with my family. I've been using my time for activities of lesser importance and haven't stopped to examine the ways I've been spending my time and to reestablish my focus.

The way I use each minute of my life affects me and those around me. It is a reflection of what I believe is most important. A month ago when I asked Jodie, a loner at school, to go to a movie with me instead of staying home to flip the channels and be bored, I felt more fulfilled and knew You were pleased. That is the kind of decision I need to make.

Please help me readjust my priorities. Give me wisdom as I choose the most important ways to use my time. I want to be so focused that when I'm faced with a decision, I make it without unnecessary reflection, confident that it is in line with my priorities.

Do you need to rethink your priorities? How can you make them more solid?

REFLECTIONS: _____

_____

_____

_____

_____

_____

_____

_____

_____

_____

_____

34

The Only Life Worth Living

But Jesus called the disciples together and said: "You know that foreign rulers like to order their people around. And their great leaders have full power over everyone they rule. But don't act like them. If you want to be great, you must be the servant of all the others. And if you want to be first, you must be the slave of the rest. The Son of Man did not come to be a slave master, but a slave who will give his life to rescue many people."

Matthew 20:25–28 CEV

I was reading on the front porch yesterday when the garbage collectors picked up our trash. They waved and said good morning, and I returned the greeting. Their job isn't an exciting one, but they seem to make the most of it.

After they left, I said to myself, "It would be neat to do something for them." I thought about it for a while and decided I'd bake each of them a bag of cookies and attach a note thanking them for being so friendly.

A week later, when they pulled onto our street, I ran out to place the cookies on top of our trash cans. Then I hurried inside and waited for them while I peeked out the window. It didn't take long for them to get to our house; and when they saw their little gifts, they looked surprised and delighted. I felt goose bumps as I watched them.

It makes me feel good to do kind things for others when they least expect it. Sometimes I clean my sister's room after she's fallen asleep because she hates to clean it and my mom is always telling her to do it. When she gets up in the morning, she runs to Mom and exclaims, "Come see my room!"

I have a neighbor who plays with his kids for hours in their backyard. One time he was giving them long rides in his wheelbarrow and the three kids next door begged, "Can we have a ride? Can we have a ride?" I could tell he was worn out, but he lifted them over the fence and pushed them all over the yard as they screamed with pleasure. He knows how satisfying it is to give of himself so others can have enjoyment.

Please help me to always remember the fun and rewarding feeling of giving of myself in small and big ways. Cultivate this desire in me to serve others uniquely and creatively. When I become self-centered, remind me that a life lived for others is the only life worth living.

Ask God to grow in you the desire to give of yourself and to show you what fun it is to live for others.

REFLECTIONS: _____

_____

_____

_____

_____

_____

_____

_____

35

College Confusion

Fear not, for I am with you;
Be not dismayed, for I am your God.
I will strengthen you,
Yes, I will help you,
I will uphold you with My righteous right hand.

Isaiah 41:10

I am sick and tired of being asked where I'm planning on going to college. Everywhere I go I feel like I'm being attacked by the same questions. "Have you decided on a college? Have you picked a major? Do you have any long-term goals? Have you made any career decisions?"

I don't know what college I want to go to, let alone what I want to do with my life. Yet I feel pressured to make up my mind now so I'll sound like I've got it all figured out and planned. Sometimes I feel like someone is standing over me ready to kick me out of the human race if I don't hurry and make up my mind concerning all this college and career confusion.

I know the adults who keep questioning me about college do so out of love for me and an interest in my life, but I wish they would remember how they felt when they were my age. Did they have their lives perfectly planned with every detail covered? As teenagers they had to make decisions that would affect their entire lives. How did they handle the pressure?

I'm glad You understand the stress, fear, and confusion

I feel each day. You don't quiz me about college and a career or warn me that I don't have much more time to decide. You know how scared I am about facing big life decisions; and You remind me that even though I'm becoming an adult, I'm still Your little child.

I want to run to You, Father. I want You to hold me and tell me it's all going to be okay and that this decision isn't as huge as it seems. Help me to rest in Your stillness, knowing that You are with me and will give me the wisdom to make the right choice about college. Thank You for being my refuge. I can run to You when all these decisions bombard me, for I feel safe in Your hiding place and I can make choices with confidence and peace.

Do you find it difficult to face "adult size" decisions as a teenager? Remember that you are still God's child and can run to Him for help anytime.

REFLECTIONS: _____

_____

_____

_____

_____

_____

_____

_____

_____

36

Stressing Out

I can do all things through Christ who strengthens me.

Philippians 4:13

Schoolwork becomes monotonous for me when I don't have the right attitude toward its demands. It becomes stressful and aggravating when I see it as work that I need to hurry up and finish so I can have some fun.

As soon as I get home from school, I dread what awaits me. I don't even enjoy my evenings anymore because I feel so pressured. If my sister wants to play Monopoly or something, I usually say, "I can't. I've got too much homework."

Most of the time, I spend more time worrying about it than I do actually getting it done. It becomes a big problem. Even my health is affected. Remember last year when I had to go to the emergency room because my stress over finals gave me intestinal problems?

Father, in spite of my attitude toward homework, I want to do my best. It brings me satisfaction when I have done a fantastic job, but sometimes I think I get too caught up in it. Schoolwork is important, I know, but I drive myself too hard. I'm so wrapped up in getting good grades and finishing an assignment that I forget the joy that comes from learning. Instead, I push myself to the limit so I can get a high grade. Father, I now realize that this is wrong. I worry too much about my schoolwork. If I will choose instead to trust You, then You will give me the strength I need to do my best!

Jesus, I can't do this work on my own strength because I have none. I'm weak and tired. You are the only One who can give me strength, the ability to pay attention, and the right attitude toward my schoolwork. I know that I can't do this homework anymore on my own because I keep on failing. So, God, please help me to do my homework. If You give me Your strength, I will be able to do it.

Do you hate doing your homework? How can you find joy and peace in doing it instead of drudgery and boredom? How can you allow God to work through you to get it done?

REFLECTIONS: _____

_____

_____

_____

_____

_____

_____

_____

_____

_____

_____

_____

37

The Outcasts

Be friendly with everyone. Don't be proud and feel that you are smarter than others. Make friends with ordinary people.

Romans 12:16 CEV

As I sat eating my lunch yesterday, surrounded by my closest friends in the school lunchroom, I happened to turn my eyes to the table where Julie was seated. She quietly sipped her milk while gazing into the busy lunchroom. Her face displayed a touch of sadness.

Only Julie sits at that table, Father, for no one wants to sit by a "nerd." She is overweight, smelly, and unattractive. Who wants to risk her reputation by associating with one of "the outcasts"? It would be embarrassing to talk to someone like that. Furthermore, one might lose friends if she dared to speak with her.

However, as I watched Julie yesterday, something strange happened that changed the way I feel about "the outcasts." I saw a part of myself in Julie, wanting love and acceptance from those around me. How deeply I long for my classmates to like me for who I am! I continued to stare at Julie with an excited awareness. I must have startled her because she abruptly turned away. I didn't see her for the rest of that day.

I've never thought of the "nerds" at school as people like me, with feelings, vulnerability, insecurity, and a need for unconditional love—a love that says "I love you for who you are."

Tomorrow I'm going to sit by Julie at lunch, Father.

I'm going to walk over there, knowing that people will stare and that my friends might laugh. I don't care; it's not them I'm trying to please.

Please give me the strength and confidence to talk to Julie tomorrow. Please also develop in me a spirit of love that looks at others and counts them as equal. Help me to love the outcasts of the world.

Ask God to show you the beauty of loving the unlovable.

REFLECTIONS: _____

_____

_____

_____

_____

_____

_____

_____

_____

_____

_____

_____

38

Heaven-Sent Friends

A man who has friends must himself be friendly,
But there is a friend who sticks closer than a brother.

Proverbs 18:24

Last week I spent the night at a close friend's house. We had such a good time remembering how we met and all the hilarious and embarrassing moments we've shared. We looked at old yearbook pictures and made fun of our goofy smiles and how we did our hair. We told each other the boys we had crushes on and laughed because now they wouldn't come close to being considered potential boyfriends.

Even though we were too giggly to think about the painful times, they too are vivid in our memories. I remember when her mom remarried. Her new husband had several kids of his own, and my friend and I talked every night as she told me how hard it was for her to live with new people. At the same time I was also having struggles at home and needed to talk to someone who understood and identified with my feelings. We depended a lot on each other during that time and couldn't have handled our situations as well without each other's help.

I love my friends and am grateful that You have placed such neat people in my life. I believe each one was put here by You to serve a purpose. Life certainly is a journey filled with different experiences, and You have given me friends who have made each one memorable.

Through my friends You have expressed Your endless

love and concern for me. When I have felt discouraged, they have said encouraging words that I know came from You. It uplifts me to know You care that much about me.

Thank You for the way You love me and communicate through the special people You have sent along my way. My life wouldn't be the same without them.

How has God used the people in your life to communicate His love?

REFLECTIONS: _____

_____

_____

_____

_____

_____

_____

_____

_____

_____

_____

_____

_____

39

When Friends Are Hurtful

Even my own familiar friend in whom I trusted,
Who ate my bread,
Has lifted up his heel against me.

Psalm 41:9

Because I've been doing a lot with the youth group at Tina's church, I've made several good friends — or I thought they were good friends. Last week I went to a concert with them and started out having one of the neatest nights of my life. I had been impressed by their devotion to You. I had thought to myself how much fun it is to go out with people who consider You their best friend.

Patrick went to the concert also. Although I tried not to show my interest in him, Susan, one of the girls in the youth group, noticed.

An hour into the concert I went to buy a T-shirt in order to beat the rush later. When I got back to my seat, all the girls were giggling. I asked them what was funny and one of them chimed, "We saved a place for you by Patrick." Someone else teased, "Did you miss Patrick while you were gone?" I knew Susan must have told them I like Patrick.

This wouldn't have been so bad if Patrick had not been standing there, hearing every word. He didn't say anything, and I cringed at the thoughts that might have been going through his head. I wanted to disappear and pretend that none of this had happened. They may have thought of their words as innocent teasing, but every word hurt me like a knife.

Even though I've only known them for a short time, I had considered them good friends. Then, all of a sudden, they mocked me as if I had no feelings. I felt humiliated and ridiculed.

Friends can be insensitive and even cruel at times. They may not realize the effect their words have. I don't think these girls did.

Help me to calm down about what happened and find comfort in You. Because I was the victim of careless speech, I've learned a lesson: consider the feelings of the other person before speaking. If I heed this lesson, I'll prevent hurting a friend as my friends hurt me.

Have you ever been hurt by a friend? What can you learn from that experience?

REFLECTIONS: _____

_____

_____

_____

_____

_____

_____

_____

_____

_____

40

Party Time

Run from temptations that capture young people. Always do the right thing. Be faithful, loving, and easy to get along with. Worship with people whose hearts are pure.

2 Timothy 2:22 CEV

Last week Katie asked me if I would like to go to her boyfriend's party. I felt apprehensive because although I trust Katie, I've never felt comfortable about Andrew. I've seen him act foolishly and rebelliously too many times. I wasn't sure I'd like his kind of party. I wanted to have fun with my friends, though, and decided to risk it.

When I arrived at the party, the music was blaring. I spotted Katie and she introduced me to several of Andrew's friends. I didn't see Andrew and asked where he was. She said she had just seen him and assumed he was fixing more snacks. After about fifteen minutes and no Andrew appeared, we started to get curious. I suggested we check the kitchen. As soon as we walked in, I told her to duck behind the kitchen counter.

"What is it?" she asked, looking confused.

"Andrew and some other guys are drunk!" I whispered emphatically. She took a peek and gasped in astonishment.

"What should we do?" She looked desperate.

"Get a new boyfriend?" I suggested sarcastically, wishing she'd see how blind she had been to stay with him.

We ended up confronting him, but our harsh words didn't penetrate. Katie was seething with anger and asked if I'd take her home. We talked for two hours at her house, and she said she was going to break up with him. "It's about time," I thought to myself, and affirmed her decision.

You taught me an important lesson that night. I had seen Andrew's behavior and knew he was a troublemaker, but chose to go to his party anyway. I should have made my choice based upon what I knew about Andrew instead of my desire to be with my friends.

When I'm asked to go to a party, please give me the discretion to make the best decision. I shouldn't choose to go only because I want to have fun with my friends. I must think about what will be going on behind the scenes. I don't want to be caught in a situation like that again. Please help me to be wise so I can avoid those situations.

How can you make the best decisions about parties?

REFLECTIONS: _____

_____

_____

_____

_____

_____

_____

_____

_____

– 41 –

Quiet Times with Jesus

O God, my heart is steadfast;
I will sing and give praise, even with my glory.
Awake, lute and harp!
I will awaken the dawn.

Psalm 108:1–2

I didn't spend time talking with You, reading the Bible, and getting life into focus this morning. I awoke and frantically began my day. I hardly thought of having my quiet time. Instead, I listed all the other things that were beckoning for my attention—chores, exercises, the remainder of my homework. I knew that in order to get them done, I couldn't spend time with You, let alone sit down and meditate.

Without my realizing it, not having a quiet time has slowly and silently become a pattern in my life. I have become overwhelmed by the rush of life and have forgotten the power and energy that results from spending some time talking with You; from reading Your Book, which guides and helps me; and from thinking about and rearranging my priorities. I have allowed the busyness of life and its pressures to blur my perception of what is most important.

Satan loves to see me discouraged so much by daily responsibilities that I give up having my quiet time altogether. He knows, too, that spending time in prayer and reflection provides spiritual power and inspiration. He is aware that when I spend time with You, he is being defeated.

Jesus, Satan has been using the pressure I feel to get things done for the purpose of distracting me. He does not want me to talk to You each day and has tricked me into believing that I don't need that contact with You.

I do need You, Jesus. I can't tackle my problems without asking for Your help each day. I have been trying to, and it doesn't work. I do need Your power and peace. I need to feel the joy of Your presence.

Please help me discipline myself to have my quiet time even when I don't feel like it, for when I do, You will strengthen and bless me. Thank You.

What changes can you make in your schedule in order to have time (or more time) to talk with your Father?

REFLECTIONS: _____

_____

_____

_____

_____

_____

_____

_____

_____

_____

42

Suicide

Remember my affliction and roaming,
The wormwood and the gall.
My soul still remembers
And sinks within me.
This I recall to my mind,
Therefore I have hope.
Through the LORD's mercies we are not consumed,
Because His compassions fail not.
They are new every morning;
Great is Your faithfulness.
"The LORD is my portion," says my soul,
"Therefore I hope in Him!"

Lamentations 3:19–24

Three high school students from my city killed themselves this year. Many people were shocked, but I wasn't. Millions of teens are severely depressed. I have been.

Father, last year was the worst year of my life. Problems at home made me feel alone and overwhelmed. I was confused and felt I had no one to talk to who fully understood the gravity of my discouragement. I didn't even feel like telling You about my feelings because I didn't think You cared. I knew in my head that You do, but I didn't believe it in my heart. I've never felt so far away from You as I did then. I felt overwhelmed by feelings of rejection and despair, and I thought the only way to alleviate my unresolved conflict was to kill myself.

I soon discovered that to want to commit suicide is to

be overcome by life's bleakness: it is to live in complete darkness. I felt as though Satan had entered my heart and flooded it with blackness. He filled my mind with suicidal thoughts, and I succumbed to their wooing.

I praise You that You saved me from death. Because many teenagers don't experience Your salvation from both physical and spiritual death, I am even more thankful.

Please protect me from any more thoughts about killing myself. When I become discouraged and distraught, remind me that crying to You for help and telling You my problems is what protects me from Satan's lies. Father, please hold on to me when I fall from You. Keep me safe and secure in Your arms.

If you are presently considering suicide as an escape, get help from a caring adult or friend as soon as possible. (This applies to your friends too.) And remember that Jesus is an ever-present help in trouble. When we cry unto Him, He hears.

REFLECTIONS: _____

_____

_____

_____

_____

_____

_____

_____

43

Lost Friends

My friends, you are spiritual. So if someone is trapped in sin, you should gently lead that person back to the right path. But watch out, and don't be tempted yourself. You obey the law of Christ when you offer each other a helping hand.

Galatians 6:1–2 CEV

I saw an old friend smoking at the mall a few weeks ago, Father. I haven't seen her for several years, but I had no idea she could change so dramatically. Her clothes were black and torn, and her eyes were sunken. She appeared to be in a daze. I stopped and stared in disbelief. The girl who used to laugh and cry with me—who always seemed to have a cheerful heart and a gentle spirit—now looked depressed and lost in the jungle of life.

I began walking toward her but stopped when a group of teenagers cussing and wearing nasty T-shirts approached her. "Those are her friends?" I cried in horror. Quickly walking away, I tried to cast her picture out of my mind. I wished I could forget what I had seen and remember her as she used to be.

It's hard to believe someone as sweet and caring as she was can become so upset by hard times that she gives up on You and turns to a life of sin. Why couldn't she have asked You for help?

I don't know what I should do, God. Should I call her? I feel as though my words couldn't penetrate her hurt and deep pain to provide the restoration and healing that she so desperately needs. I want to help, but how? Maybe I will call her after all and ask if she wants to get together to talk. That would provide a chance for You to communicate Your love and concern for her through me.

Do you know someone who has lost his way? What can you do to help?

REFLECTIONS: _____

_____

_____

_____

_____

_____

_____

_____

_____

_____

_____

_____

_____

_____

_____

44

Just Say No

The Lord will guide you continually,
And satisfy your soul in drought,
And strengthen your bones;
You shall be like a watered garden,
And like a spring of water, whose waters do not fail.

Isaiah 58:11

One of the women whose kids I sometimes take care of called and asked me to baby-sit tonight. Her older daughter is in the hospital, and she needs to go see her. I knew I couldn't because I've got tons of work to do, but I said yes anyway because I didn't want to feel guilty for turning her down. Besides, her daughter is sick. To say I couldn't help her would sound insensitive.

Now I feel frustrated because I'm overloaded with work. How will I ever get it done with all this baby-sitting? I need every minute to finish it, and now three hours are chopped out of the picture because I told myself I had to say yes to the baby-sitting job. I don't know what I'm going to do.

Why do I always feel that I have to say yes to everyone who asks me to do something? I have a desire to help and care for others, but I think I help other people too much. I tell myself it's selfish not to take care of their needs. It's hard for me to realize that I've got a life too and that thinking about my needs to get work done or to have time by myself or with my family is important.

Help me to be able to say no in a kind but firm way.

Please help me not to get so wrapped up in others' needs that I neglect my own. Teach me how to take care of myself and how to balance it with taking care of others. Thank You for being aware of my needs even when I'm not.

Do you feel guilty when you tell people you can't help them? How does God want you to view your needs?

REFLECTIONS: _____

_____

_____

_____

_____

_____

_____

_____

_____

_____

_____

_____

_____

_____

— 45 —

Embracing the Pain

And we know that all things work together for good to those who love God, to those who are the called according to His purpose.

Romans 8:28

I talked today with a friend whose sister, Laura, has diabetes. She is in the sixth grade and is a sweet and gentle girl who lives with a difficult situation.

We got into a lengthy discussion about the hard times their family has gone through because of the danger of the disease. She said Laura must always keep her blood sugar level stabilized because a coma could result if it gets too low or too high. In order to keep it balanced, she gives herself two shots of insulin and takes five blood samples a day by pricking her finger. In addition, she has a strict diet and must eat at certain times of day.

I can't imagine living like that. Tiring easily, being forced to stop whatever you're doing in order to drink a bit of apple juice so your body can function, hassling with shots and pricks, and living with the danger of the disease would be hard. I admire Laura because she has adjusted and learned how to incorporate the disease into her life without letting it ruin her spirit. The ongoing difficulty of it has shaped an unusual strength within her.

Thinking about Laura's life has revealed something to me about mine. I have been going through a hard time and haven't wanted to accept my pain. I've tried to push it away, ignore it, and deny it. I haven't been able to see my hurt as Laura sees her diabetes and accept it, even though my heart may cry, "Go away! I don't need you and don't want you." Rather than confronting it, I have walked away.

In not dealing with my hurt feelings, I have unknowingly allowed them to chew me up like a vulture eating its prey. My denial has produced what I have been trying to prevent: intensified feelings of pain.

I need to acknowledge my hurt and not resist it. I don't want to live with the pain because it feels horrible, but I now see that I must in order for You to use it and, in Your time, heal it.

Help me to accept this hard time and to rest in the fact that You will use it for my good. Transform these feelings of hurt into something beautiful. Give me the strength not only to acknowledge my pain, but to embrace it.

When you go through a hard time, do you try to ignore or deny painful feelings? How can you deal with them in a healthy way?

REFLECTIONS: _____

_____

_____

_____

_____

_____

_____

_____

46

Reaping What I Don't Mow

Do not be deceived, God is not mocked; for whatever a man sows, that he will also reap.

Galatians 6:7

I didn't mow the yard last Saturday because I goofed off by sleeping late, going to the mall, and seeing a movie. I thought I could fit it in somewhere, but I didn't make much of an effort. When I got home it was too late. When I mowed and clipped today, there was so much grass that I bagged up twice as much as I usually do.

I was mad because the mower kept dying; it could barely get through the grass. Also, I had grass clippings in my shoes, and my arms and legs were speckled. Then the gas ran out and I had to stop, clean off, and go buy some more. When I came back, the sun was shining brightly and it was hot and steamy. It took me three hours to finish mowing, and then I had to trim the weeds. Finally, after having worked all morning and part of the afternoon, I finished. I was too exhausted to be angry.

If I had mowed last week as I was supposed to, the yard wouldn't have been such a hassle today. I was too mad to realize this earlier, but now I do. I should have managed my time more wisely so this could have been prevented. If I had known what a pain it was going to be to do the yard today, I probably would have found the time to do it.

When I choose not to do what I'm supposed to, unpleasant consequences result. I need to realize the power of my will—my ability to choose between right and wrong. When bad consequences result from wrong choices, I usually try to rationalize my decisions and deny the fact that I didn't choose what was best. I seldom tell myself, "You reap what you sow."

When I'm faced with a decision, give me the wisdom to consider the consequences. Help me to be a responsible teenager who makes wise choices. Then I'll be much happier with the results.

Before making a decision, do you stop and consider the consequences? What are some ways you can keep yourself accountable for the choices you make?

REFLECTIONS: _____

_____

_____

_____

_____

_____

_____

_____

_____

_____

_____

47

Embarrassing Moments

[Be] hospitable, a lover of what is good, sober-minded, just, holy, self-controlled.

Titus 1:8

My mom embarrassed me today—again. We were at a bookstore and I saw a book I've wanted for a long time. I asked her if she'd buy it and said I'd pay her back the next day.

When we got to the cashier, she started digging through her purse. I asked what the problem was, and she said she couldn't find a check. The cashier had already rung up the book and was waiting anxiously because there were people in line behind us. I plunged my hands into her purse and dug through it myself, but with the same result. My mom apologized to the cashier, and as we left I gave my mom an exasperated look.

When we got outside I said through clenched teeth, "Why did you have to embarrass me like that? Everyone in line was staring at us! You could at least have a clean purse so we wouldn't have had to scramble through all that junk." She apologized for embarrassing me, and after we got home I started to feel guilty about getting mad.

It seems that everywhere I go with my mom or dad, they do something that embarrasses me. Sometimes I try to stop them by giving them the look that says, "You're humiliating me." I always say something afterward. Then they get frustrated and respond sarcastically, "Well, we can't say anything right these days."

Help me see things from my parents' perspective a little better. Many times my mom has said she doesn't realize that her words and actions embarrass me. She explains that she thinks differently and is trying to see things from my point of view. I wish I wouldn't get angry at her and my dad. I need to have more self-control when expressing my feelings.

Help me to realize that my mom and dad are people who make mistakes too. I need to learn to express my feelings of embarrassment without making them feel bad. Then we can talk about the situation in order to prevent it from happening again.

What can you do to prevent embarrassing moments from occurring and to control your anger when they do?

REFLECTIONS: _____

_____

_____

_____

_____

_____

_____

_____

_____

_____

48

Risking Humility

Always be humble and gentle. Patiently put up with each other and love each other.

Ephesians 4:2 CEV

At lunch today a boy spilled his food on the floor. It made a huge mess, especially the spaghetti. Several noodles stuck to his face, and some of the sauce splashed onto a girl's slacks. Because his tray made a loud noise when it fell, everyone in the lunchroom turned to see what the commotion was. His face was as red as a tomato and he stood there, not knowing what to do.

After looking around in embarrassment for quite some time, he made several apologies to the girl on whose slacks he'd spilled spaghetti sauce. Then he peeled the noodles off his face. Everyone laughed hysterically as he attempted to clean up the slop. I was standing in line behind him and thought, "I should help him." No one else was helping.

I didn't want to get anything on my clothes, but I decided to risk that. His face lit up when I reached down to wipe the mess off the floor. I got spaghetti sauce on my shirt, but I didn't care because of the smile of gratitude on his face.

Later that day a teacher stopped me in the hall and commended me for helping him. She said it was unselfish of me to get down on my hands and knees while everyone in the lunchroom watched. Her compliment made me realize there is truth in the verse that says it's "more blessed to give than receive."

Father, I'm willing to help those in need even though it's hard sometimes; I don't want to risk being laughed at. However, if that is the risk, let me do it with no less enthusiasm.

Thank You for teaching me about humility today. Please continue to show me its attractiveness. I want humility to characterize every act and every word of mine. I want it in my life because a humble heart makes You happy.

Is it hard for you to be humble when risks are involved? How can you make it easier to choose humility?

REFLECTIONS: _____

_____

_____

_____

_____

_____

_____

_____

_____

_____

_____

_____

– 49 –

Obsessions

Direct my steps by Your word,
And let no iniquity have dominion over me.

Psalm 119:133

I feel I'm messed up because many times I overeat to make myself feel better when I am hurt or confused. Sometimes I feel so depressed about a huge test that I come home the day before, open the refrigerator, and gobble up everything in sight. When I am mad at my parents, I grab the cookie jar and stuff my face, not even tasting the cookies.

Father, I pray with all my heart that You will not allow me to become addicted to food. As I examine myself now, I see the lack of control I have over my body. I see that something is definitely wrong. Each day my overeating is becoming more and more obvious. This habit is becoming ingrained—hardened—into my way of life. It is blinding me to the truth that You are the One I need to turn to when I am hurt. Yet I find myself depending on food. This craving tells me to come to it when I feel sad, and I say okay. So I turn to food again and again, but I cannot turn any more! I know I can't or I'll become Miss Fat Woman. Then my self-image will plunge into the depths, and I will feel far away from You.

Oh, please help me! Help me to center on You to overcome this craving. Don't let me give in to this bad habit! Show me what I am trying to satisfy—maybe a lonely or depressed heart or the emptiness of broken dreams.

Please help me to establish helpful ways of dealing with overwhelming emotions, such as calling a friend, talking with my mom, or going for a walk and telling You about my feelings.

Father, free me from this habit that has the potential of becoming an obsession if I don't do something about it right now. Give me the maturity and strength to face my problems and to conquer them so I may have freedom from these chains.

Do you have bad habits? What needs are you trying to fill up or satisfy? How do you think God can help you find freedom from these chains? Ask for His help.

REFLECTIONS: _____

_____

_____

_____

_____

_____

_____

_____

_____

_____

_____

50

Battles

Dear friends, I urge you, as aliens and strangers in the world, to abstain from sinful desires, which war against your soul.

1 Peter 2:11 NIV

The sky was strange today. At first it was filled with black and gray clouds, but then they suddenly moved away and the sun burst through the blur. This happened again and again throughout the day: the light penetrated the dark, and the dark fought back.

When the rainclouds covered the sunshine, the light rays shining on my bedroom walls turned into dull shadows, making my room dark and gloomy. When the sunlight shone back through, however, it was like a playful dance bouncing on the walls.

I saw myself in the sky today. Like the sun fighting the rainclouds, the good part of me battles the bad. I sin, do something good, and sin again. I can't count on myself to be consistent in doing what's right. When I think I'm doing a pretty terrific job, I blow it and fall flat on my face.

When I became a Christian, You gave me a new life. You declared me righteous and blameless instead of dirty and guilty as I was before. Yet my old nature is still present in me because I can choose to live out of my new life or my old life — my old nature with all its harmful desires and patterns.

I'm sick of giving in to my old nature. It's always present, tempting me and promising me there's more pleasure in giving in to my sinful desires than there is in choosing to do right.

Help me understand this battle within me so I can fight with Your skill and strength. I need You to be my Commander and Defender so we can fight the darkness together.

Do you get tired of fighting your sinful desires? How can you win the battles that rage within?

REFLECTIONS: _____

_____

_____

_____

_____

_____

_____

_____

_____

_____

_____

_____

_____

_____

51

Staring into Adulthood

Rejoice, O young man, in your youth,
And let your heart cheer you in the days of your youth;
Walk in the ways of your heart,
And in the sight of your eyes;
But know that for all these
God will bring you into judgment.
Therefore remove sorrow from your heart,
And put away evil from your flesh,
For childhood and youth are vanity.

Ecclesiastes 11:9–10

It's scary to think about becoming an adult. I've been a kid all this time, and now adulthood is coming closer and closer. It's a phase of my life that seems adventurous but almost overwhelming. Sometimes I feel that I'll never get there, but other times I want to push it away because it seems too close.

As a child I was safe and sheltered. I didn't worry about adult matters. I'd play all day with my neighborhood friends without being concerned about making money and plans for the future. Now I have jobs and bigger responsibilities. I have to think about how the decisions I make at this time will affect my adult life.

Sometimes I want to be a teenager forever. Going to movies with my friends, playing volleyball with good-looking guys at the pool, lying around the house with nothing to do, and riding around town with the music playing are what make being a teenager fun. I guess we're trying to live it up before the responsibilities of adulthood stifle our free spirits.

I need to approach adulthood from a more positive point of view. I will enjoy it if I live the dreams I want for that stage of life.

Please help me to plan wisely for the future, but to enjoy being a teenager. I need to find a balance. Help me to enjoy living one day at a time.

How can you look forward to being an adult without worry and fear?

REFLECTIONS: _____

_____

_____

_____

_____

_____

_____

_____

_____

_____

_____

52

Selfless Trust

Trust in the LORD with all your heart,
And lean not on your own understanding.

Proverbs 3:5

I'm on a school trip and am on a different bus than all my friends. The majority of the kids on my bus are a lot younger than I am. They're wild and hyper. I feel as though I'm being surrounded by a cluster of swarming bees. I don't want to be here!

The kids around me are enjoying themselves. They have their friends. All I have is my favorite book!

I can imagine my friends now—laughing, singing senseless songs, having a super time. And here I sit, staring out the window, watching the endless rain fall, and wishing I could join them.

I feel alone and left out. If only I could jump out of this bus and hop on the other one! I could be with *them* and take part in what they're doing. These kids are with their friends. Why can't I be with mine?

Sometimes what I plan is not Your plan. It is often difficult to accept Your will with a willing and cheerful heart. I am eager to have my wishes and plans fulfilled, but not so eager to be a part of Your plan when it goes against my personal desires.

It hurts to relinquish my desires for Your higher ones. When my plans do not work out, I seldom exclaim, "Oh, that's OK. I just want to do what You want me to do, God." It's hard to trust that Your plans are greater than mine.

Help me to be willing to do what You want. Please help me to trust You even when Your will contradicts mine. I love You and want to embrace Your desires with strength until mine become Yours.

When something you planned doesn't turn out as you thought it would, how can you handle your disappointment? Would trusting in God make a difference in how you react?

REFLECTIONS: _____

_____

_____

_____

_____

_____

_____

_____

_____

_____

_____

_____

_____

_____

Being a Young Woman

For You formed my inward parts;
You covered me in my mother's womb.
I will praise You, for I am fearfully and wonderfully made;
Marvelous are Your works,
And that my soul knows very well.

Psalm 139:13–14

Today is hot and steamy. I sweat if I just walk from one room to the next. I can't stand this weather! Also, I'm having my period today and I don't feel well. My stomach hurts. I know I'm irritable because a friend just called to ask for help with a homework question and I coldly responded, "I don't know the answer. Why would I know?"

My emotions go up and down continually when this time comes around. I become grouchy and sulky. My family agrees! Yesterday my mom asked me to fold the towels and I screamed, "No! I don't want to fold the stupid towels!" Most of the time, I don't even know why I'm angry or suddenly down in the dumps. I sure wish I could understand what is happening to my body. I don't know what causes my emotions to jump up and down as they do at this time. Maybe I'm making a big deal out of all these changes, but I get so frustrated.

Father, You made me this way, and I know that You delight in Your creations. You are pleased with the way You made us. Please show me Your delight, so I may also delight in this stage of my life. I am Your daughter, and I want to be happy when You, my Father, are happy. I want to be pleased with my body and all that is happening to it because You are. When days like today come, help me not to feel so frustrated.

Perhaps being a young woman is more special than I realize. I guess being able to give birth to a life and to have the mothering qualities that a new life needs is pretty neat, now that I think about it. Yes, I suppose young womanhood is a special and unique stage of life that I should enjoy. I'll try to see it that way.

How can you get beyond your aggravation on days like this? What can you do to help this time of life seem not just more endurable, but actually pleasurable?

REFLECTIONS: _____

_____

_____

_____

_____

_____

_____

_____

_____

_____

_____

54

Refreshing Rain

Now the Lord is the Spirit; and where the Spirit of the Lord is, there is liberty.

2 Corinthians 3:17

Today You watered the earth with Your rain. I felt renewed as I watched it fall faster and faster on the green grass. I listened to its quiet splashes on our driveway and thought that through its quietness, You were showing me You love me simply because I am Your creation. Then after the rain stopped, my sister and I splashed in its puddles. I squealed as she kicked the water onto my face and hair.

We went stomping in the puddles all the way down the street, laughing with joy. Then I sat down on the curb and let the water rush over my feet. It was ice cold, but I didn't care. I felt free because I was being childish and crazy. Yet I wasn't concerned about what anyone around thought of me. All my worries about life vanished! I wasn't disturbed about my flabby thighs, about the trash waiting to be taken out, or about the newly arrived pimple on my face. I felt free.

I ran around dancing like a child, and I didn't care who saw me. I leaned my head back and let the cool rain fall onto my face. I started singing loudly just as my sister hates for me to do. I sang stupid songs, and it was tons of fun.

Later, when I took a soothing, hot shower, I stood there thinking of how You take care of us through the rain. I thought of how the rain makes my grandpa's wheat grow and my mom's pretty flowers bloom. New plants sprout, bringing new life.

I thought of how You are like the rain, making me happy when I feel sad and dried up like a desert. Yes, You are like the rain, refreshing me, causing me to grow and become stronger, and bringing me new life. You remind me that You are the One who gives me eternal life in Heaven because Your Son chose to die on a cross to save me from death. Thank You for reminding me through the rain of my new life!

Thank You for coming when my soul is dry, dry, dry, and making it wet. Just when I need You, You come and bring me joy and freedom. Oh, how awesome is Your liberty when all my worries are washed away, and You set my eyes only on You! Then I become a young child, dazzled by the greatness of Your love.

Do you sometimes feel bound up inside by all your worries? Who can give you freedom? Ask Jesus to wash away your anxieties with His refreshing rain.

REFLECTIONS: _____

_____

_____

_____

_____

_____

_____

_____

55

When God Feels Distant

Now this is the confidence that we have in Him, that if we ask anything according to His will, He hears us.

1 John 5:14

Sometimes I feel that You're far away and don't hear me. It seems as though my prayers don't pass the ceiling. I pray and feel no different afterward. I wish You would give me some kind of assurance that You've heard my words. They are spoken with deep feeling and a longing to be touched by Your presence. I need a response of some kind. Why have I felt empty lately after having talked to You?

I have questions I want answers to and problems I want acknowledged. The Bible says that You know all about me and that You hear my cries, but I don't believe it with my heart. My problems are still here with equal intensity, and my questions are still unanswered. I'm starting to have doubts that You even care about me here on Planet Earth. Why can't I feel Your concern and Your love? God, can You hear me?

Lately I've felt that I'm wandering through a jungle and am calling out to You for help and direction. But You're not responding, so I keep walking, feeling alone, afraid, and lost.

You've answered my prayers in unmistakable ways in the past. Can't You do that now? I only want to know that You hear my cries and that You care.

I'm having a difficult time believing what the Bible says

about Your neverending love for me and Your concern for my problems. I desperately need You to help me trust the promises that You'll never leave me but will strengthen and protect me.

Help me to learn to trust what the Bible says and not to let my feelings tell me what's true and what's not. I need to learn to depend on Your words and not rely completely on my feelings.

Do you sometimes feel that God is far away and doesn't hear or care about you? What does the Bible say about His feelings toward you and His promises?

REFLECTIONS: _____

_____

_____

_____

_____

_____

_____

_____

_____

_____

_____

_____

Laughing at Life

And Sarah said, "God has made me laugh, and all who hear will laugh with me."

Genesis 21:6

I went skiing with my youth group last week. We stayed at a nice lodge and had our "get-togethers" in a cozy room equipped with sofas and a fireplace. I was amazed at how many teenagers had come—the largest number to come on one of our youth trips.

One evening we had an unusually serious and meaningful time as our youth group leader talked about accepting one another. I had chosen not to go to the bathroom before the meeting started and thought I could wait until it was over, but toward the end I knew I couldn't make it. I quietly left the room; and when I got back, I noticed several people staring at my shoe and snickering. I looked down and to my dismay found a long piece of toilet paper stuck to the bottom of my shoe. What it must have looked like to waltz in with toilet paper trailing behind me like a streamer! Eventually the entire group was laughing. As I thought of how ridiculous the situation was, I started laughing too.

Life is filled with embarrassing moments, but to laugh at them makes them enjoyable instead of painfully humiliating. To look back on them as funny times cheers my soul.

I need to learn how to laugh at life. I often take it too seriously and don't see the light side. The Bible says You laugh, so I might as well laugh too! Thank You for the gift of laughter. It is like a healing ointment for a heavy heart.

Do you take life too seriously? If so, how can you learn to see the bright side of life?

REFLECTIONS: _____

_____

_____

_____

_____

_____

_____

_____

_____

_____

_____

_____

_____

_____

57

Marriage in This Generation

If any of you lacks wisdom, let him ask of God, who gives to all liberally and without reproach, and it will be given to him.

James 1:5

My parents told me that some good friends of ours are getting a divorce. They said they've been having problems for about five years but have never let anyone see their struggle. We've known them for a long time and never sensed any tension between them, so to hear the news was a shock.

It seems that everyone is divorced. It's almost a surprise to meet a married couple who has been married to only each other. Divorce is so common that to see an intact family is refreshing.

Spouse abuse is also prevalent. It is a silent tragedy that pervades our country and destroys families. I have witnessed four cases of it. When I was a child, I watched in horror as our next-door neighbor tried to run over his wife with his truck. The men get out of control and the women don't know what to do. If they try to escape, will their husbands beat them or try to kill them? They live in fear, and their children grow up in an environment not much better than hell.

With even my small amount of knowledge of divorce and spouse abuse, it's hard not to have doubts about marriage. If divorce and spouse abuse rates are high now, what will they be like when I decide to get married?

I don't want to get a divorce, and I definitely don't want to be abused. How can I be sure that neither of these things will happen? Lots of women don't realize they're marrying a violent person or someone from whom they'll later be divorced after countless fights and disagreements.

Please give me wisdom in my relationships with guys my age and older men because those relationships form my ideas of what I want and don't want in a husband. Help me perceive behaviors such as a quick temper and a domineering attitude so I can be warned of potential danger in my dating relationships.

I'll need Your direction when the time comes to marry. I'm afraid I'll make the wrong choice. Help me to recognize the person You've chosen for me. Give me careful eyes to pick up on danger signs and a strong heart to do what's best.

It is vital that you pick the right husband. What are some qualities you're looking for in the person you marry?

REFLECTIONS: _____

_____

_____

_____

_____

_____

58

Taking a Stand

Remember Jesus Christ, raised from the dead, descended from David. This is my gospel, for which I am suffering even to the point of being chained like a criminal. But God's word is not chained.

2 Timothy 2:8–9 NIV

On our way to New Mexico to do mission work last week, a lot of the people in my youth group kept cussing and taking Your name in vain. It seemed ludicrous that we were on a trip to serve You as examples of Your love to people who were poor and needy. Those who weren't using Your name disrespectfully sat there as if nothing were happening. No one seemed bothered by it except me.

A bunch of thoughts ran through my head. "If they don't stop in ten minutes, I'll say something," I determined. "But what if they laugh at me and think I'm acting like a baby? I'd be humiliated. They'll probably get mad and avoid me the rest of the week. They might even talk about me behind my back and call me a goody-goody. Maybe I shouldn't say anything."

After thinking about it for quite a while, I decided to say something to them, even though I knew they'd probably think it was stupid. I was more scared than I've been in a long time, but I blurted, "I don't want you all to think I'm trying to be super spiritual, but I don't think it's right to use God's name the way you are. I think He deserves more respect than that."

There was silence for several seconds, and a couple of people said they were sorry. I was so nervous I was shaking, but I felt good about taking a stand.

Thank You for giving me courage that day. I don't regret saying what I did, even though a few people seemed annoyed.

Give me the boldness to stand up for my beliefs in a humble way. The last thing I want to do is alienate my friends, but I might if I want to be strong in my faith. Please help me to stand up and not be afraid.

When someone does something that contradicts your beliefs, how do you handle it? Are you willing to take a risk and perhaps suffer for Christ? Read 2 Corinthians 11:24–28.

REFLECTIONS: _____

_____

_____

_____

_____

_____

_____

_____

_____

_____

59

Apart from the World

Do not love the world or the things in the world. If anyone loves the world, the love of the Father is not in him. For all that is in the world—the lust of the flesh, the lust of the eyes, and the pride of life—is not of the Father but is of the world. And the world is passing away, and the lust of it; but he who does the will of God abides forever.

1 John 2:15–17

The movie was about to begin. I squirmed in my seat as my friends shared their favorite scenes. They had seen it once before and couldn't wait to see it again. I wasn't sure I wanted to see this one. I had heard some bad reports, yet had decided to go because of my friends' persuasion. "You'll love it," they assured me.

The opening scene turned out to be okay. It was even funny in some parts. As the movie continued, though, the bad language worsened, and the star of the show turned out to be a prostitute. After several bed scenes I knew why I had had qualms about going. I endured the rest and inwardly vowed I'd never again go to a movie about which I had heard bad reports—even if my friends gave rave reviews.

It is easy to get caught up in the lust of the world. We are often blinded to the world's depravity and evil way of living. Satan makes sin look harmless. It may be pleasurable for a short time, but the results are a guilty conscience—a realization that I have fallen from Your standard—and a dirty feeling in my heart.

I must be continually attentive and alert in order to stay away from Satan's traps. He wants me to fall into the world's thinking and behavior patterns, but I can't because he is not my master.

Please help me to stay completely unspoiled by the world. Every day I am tempted to follow its ways of living. It is difficult not to give in to its passions. I need Your power to resist.

How can you remain separate from the world while living in it?

REFLECTIONS: _____

_____

_____

_____

_____

_____

_____

_____

_____

_____

_____

60

A Mind Like Christ's

Finally, brethren, whatever things are true, whatever things are noble, whatever things are just, whatever things are pure, whatever things are lovely, whatever things are of good report, if there is any virtue and if there is anything praiseworthy— meditate on these things.

Philippians 4:8

I watched a video of my favorite song this afternoon on MTV. It wasn't perverted or violent, but the next few were. I planned on turning the TV off after I saw the one I wanted to watch, but I decided to relax some more. I kept it on without realizing what a bad mistake I was making.

The videos weren't horrendous as far as videos go, but they weren't something I'd see in Sunday school either. They made the relationship between a man and a woman look like a joke, and sex seemed to be something you do with anyone and everyone.

It's easy to get caught up in watching bad videos. They're enticing; they pull my mind into another world, away from reality. It's hard to turn the TV off when I'm being sucked into that kind of atmosphere.

I can't believe how much garbage I've put in my mind by watching that stuff. It's not easy to wash away the pictures they leave in my memory because they're vivid and powerful.

Maybe I shouldn't watch MTV at all. There are some decent videos, but most of them are junky. If I don't allow myself to watch any of them, it won't be as easy to fall into the temptation of watching the crummy ones.

Help me to realize the importance of filling my mind with good pictures and ideas. If I set my mind on heavenly thoughts and not on the thoughts of the world, I will be more able to think like Jesus. Give me the power to do that. I want my mind to become like Christ's even though it seems hard.

Think about what you see on TV. Is there something you shouldn't be watching?

REFLECTIONS: _____

_____

_____

_____

_____

_____

_____

_____

_____

_____

_____

_____

_____

61

Painting on Masks

An honest person tells the truth in court, but a dishonest person tells nothing but lies.

Proverbs 12:17 CEV

A friend gave me a note today that surprised me and woke me up to a common situation at our age. In the note she explained that her smiling face at school does not reflect what she feels inside. She said that at home her mom constantly yells at her and accuses her of things she didn't do, and her dad does nothing to stop it. "I want to please people—to make them like me—so I smile and act happy even though I'm hurting on the inside," she wrote.

The note shocked me because I've always seen her laughing and happy. Her demeanor looked genuine, and I had no idea it was a cover-up for her true feelings. I wrote her back, assuring her that lots of people wear masks over their pain. "I've done it many times," I confessed.

Almost everyone pretends at times. Sometimes it's obvious when someone's being fake, but often it's not detectable. We're good at hiding our true feelings and painting on the faces we think others want to see. When people ask, "How are you today?" we usually respond, "Fine." No one is fine all the time. I wonder if anyone has truthfully responded with, "Actually, I'm going through a hard time, but I'm hangin' in there." We don't have to announce our problems to the world, but we could at least be honest when people ask.

Help me to be truthful about my feelings. When I feel like crying, don't let me paint on a smile instead. Help me not to lie about what's going on in my deepest thoughts, but to be honest when someone asks me how I'm doing. Take away my mask, and give me the courage to be real.

Do you hide your deep-down feelings? What are the benefits of being honest about them?

REFLECTIONS: _____

_____

_____

_____

_____

_____

_____

_____

_____

_____

_____

_____

_____

_____

Music's Impact

He has delivered us from the power of darkness and conveyed us into the kingdom of the Son of His love.

Colossians 1:13

Some of the music I listen to isn't the best. My tapes and CDs are fine; it's the radio that sometimes plays the rotten stuff. I've grown so used to the bad songs that I often sing along. I've started to realize this is wrong. The lyrics get in my head and feed ungodly thoughts into my memory.

It's easy to get sucked into the bad songs on the radio. I don't turn it on thinking, "Oh, goody. I'm going to listen to some bad songs." I listen to them because I like the beat or because they're mixed in with the good ones. I've become so desensitized to the words that I hardly notice the meaning.

However, while I was boppin' around my room yesterday, I started thinking about the words. I began to realize that I shouldn't listen to that kind of song. I started thinking, "I can't believe I've gotten sucked into these songs. I've been listening to this music without realizing how destructive it is to my mind."

Music has an effect on me. Certain secular songs put thoughts into my mind that create a distorted mind-set and dangerous attitudes. One song I used to listen to repeated many times, "Nothing really matters to me." After listening to the words, I felt discouraged; and it's no wonder. Who could have a positive outlook on life after listening to a man cry out that life has no meaning?

Thank You for making me aware of what I've been doing. I'm glad You showed me how unhealthy it is to listen to some of today's secular music. Starting over will be tough, but I'm going to try my best. I need to choose the best secular songs and listen to tapes that will fill my mind with uplifting thoughts instead of destructive ones. That way I'll become more like You, the source of light, and less like the world.

Is the music you listen to the kind that God wants to fill your mind?

REFLECTIONS: _____

_____

_____

_____

_____

_____

_____

_____

_____

_____

_____

_____

63

Making Dreams Come True

But He is unique, and who can make Him change?
And whatever His soul desires, that He does.

Job 23:13

Boris Yeltsin is one of my heroes. Of all the well-known people I've read about, he is one of the most daring, determined, and motivated. In his autobiography he told the story of his excursion to the woods (as a teenager) to find the source of a river with his friends.

After walking for several weeks, they finally reached their destination. They started home but were too worn out to walk, so they gathered some of their possessions, took them to the owner of a cottage nearby, and traded them for a small boat. On their way down the river they spotted a cave and decided to explore it. They walked on and on until the cave opened into one of the deepest parts of the forest. They were lost and barely found enough to eat. To quench their thirst, they drank swamp water.

Eventually they found the river and their boat and they started back home. However, the swamp water made them so sick they passed out. When they were found, they were taken to the hospital where they stayed for almost three months.

Thank goodness he survived because he turned out to be an influential man of reform. Boris Yeltsin's drive and hard work have liberated a land from the grip of Communism. The risks he has taken and his fierce determination have made him a leader and a fighter. Unstoppable, he has made his dreams reality.

I long to seize my dreams like Boris Yeltsin. I don't want them to die: I want to give them life. I couldn't stand living my life without a dream—something for which to fight, dare, risk my reputation, and seize. I'd rather die today having grasped my dreams than live until I'm ninety without even trying to make them happen.

I want my life to be as awesome as I can make it. I don't want to fade into obscurity but to rise up and show what You can do through me. You have placed these dreams in me, and they are worth risking all I've got.

Give me energy every moment of the day to move toward my dreams. Make them stronger until they burn within me. Life is short, and I need the strength and determination to use every minute. Give me the ambition and the focus to make my dreams reality.

Ask God for the inspiration to make your dreams come true.

REFLECTIONS: _____

_____

_____

_____

_____

_____

_____

Story taken from *Against the Grain: The Autobiography of Boris Yeltsin* (New York: Summit Books, 1990).

64

The Boyfriend Stealer

You will be secure, because there is hope;
you will look about you and take your rest in safety.
You will lie down, with no one to make you afraid,
and many will court your favor.

Job 11:18–19 NIV

The girl who sat in front of me last night at church talked and laughed with her friends throughout the service. A guest speaker had come to speak to us teens, and she and the people sitting next to her had come from a church out of town to hear him.

She kept flinging her hair and giggling until it became a distraction for those sitting behind her. I wondered why she was acting weird. Then I saw her turn her head and glance directly at Patrick. I thought, "So that's why you're making such a racket. You're trying to get the attention of *my* boyfriend."

She had the boldness to turn around and look at him three more times. I felt like steam was coming out of my ears. The third time I gave her a nasty look. If looks could kill, she would have been a goner.

I couldn't believe how angry I was. I didn't even hear the rest of the message. I felt like telling "Miss Blonde Hair and Blue Eyes" to find her own boyfriend.

I know the reason I was upset is because I feel insecure. I'm scared Patrick will leave me and find another girl. Wherever we go together, I scout the area for girls who would love to steal him from me.

Please help me to loosen up and not be so insecure that I hurt the level of trust in my relationship with him. Help me to talk to him about my feeling of insecurity. Thank You for this special person in my life.

Are you involved in a relationship in which you feel insecure? Have you talked to your boyfriend about this feeling?

REFLECTIONS: _____

_____

_____

_____

_____

_____

_____

_____

_____

_____

_____

_____

_____

_____

_____

65

Treasured Memories

I have fought the good fight, I have finished the race, I have kept the faith.

2 Timothy 4:7

Today is the last day before my senior year of high school starts. I went to the park nearby to enjoy it because the temperature was only eighty-two degrees. I thought it would be a good idea to sit and reflect for a while.

As I sat against one of the big oak trees, the wind blew softly and lifted my hair away from my face. The afternoon was beautiful, and the peaceful atmosphere stimulated my thoughts. I reflected on the fun, relaxing vacations I had taken and how much better I felt about starting school this year than the last two because I had truly relaxed this time. I'm glad I did because I'll be spending next summer getting ready for college.

As I thought about how to make this last year of high school special, I was amazed at how fast my life has gone. One day I'm painting Easter eggs with my five-year-old friends, and the next day I'm getting senior pictures taken. It seems like yesterday I was asking my mom if I could shave my legs like the other girls in my class. Now it's a pain.

Memories from my childhood flooded my mind. Most were pleasant, but some were sad. I remembered the time a stray kitten I had decided to keep was killed by the neighbor's dog. I cried for days. I also remembered my first boyfriend, the birth of my sister, and the time I met my best friend. I vowed, "I will treasure these memories as long as I live."

Now I'm almost an adult and I realize how short life is. I want to make memories *now* that I'll cherish. When I'm older and about to die, I want to look back on my life and be pleased with the memories and satisfied with the way I lived my life.

Life is short. How can you fill it with good memories?

REFLECTIONS: _____

_____

_____

_____

_____

_____

_____

_____

_____

_____

_____

66

The Unseen World

Put on the whole armor of God, that you may be able to stand against the wiles of the devil. For we do not wrestle against flesh and blood, but against principalities, against powers, against the rulers of the darkness of this age, against spiritual hosts of wickedness in the heavenly places.

Ephesians 6:11–12

My mom and I have been fascinated by the spiritual warfare class we've been taking for the past two months. Learning about the spiritual realm has brought me into Your world with keener eyes and a steadier heart. It has opened a world of which I've never been fully aware. Learning about the fights between angels and demons and how each battle impacts my relationship to You has given me the drive to resist Satan's attacks.

Until I started taking this class, I never realized how real the spiritual world is. On a date I'd be tempted to go further and further, and I'd hear my mind saying no. I didn't see the underlying conflict between Your angels and Satan's demons as the angels fought for my purity and the demons tried to drag me away from my salvation to my destruction. I didn't realize the invisible battles taking place every minute of the day. I perceived reality through my physical eyes and not my spiritual ones.

I don't understand a lot about the spiritual realm, but I'm learning more each day. The angels protect, defend, and encourage me, and I too must fight in the battle with my belt of truth, vest of righteousness, shield of faith, helmet of salvation, and sword of the Spirit—the Bible.

You've given me the strength to be victorious in the war against Satan, even though I lose countless battles. You've made me a warrior so that I may learn to use the truth of the Bible, the Holy Spirit, Your unending grace, and my will to do what's right, though Satan desperately tries to entice me into wrongdoing.

Continue to give me insight into the power of the spiritual realm. Make me a brave warrior—one who intimidates Satan himself—in the unseen world.

How can you be more in touch with the spiritual world?

REFLECTIONS: _____

_____

_____

_____

_____

_____

_____

_____

_____

_____

_____

67

Thinking for Myself

If you want to live, give up your foolishness and let under-standing guide your steps.

Proverbs 9:6 CEV

Today in Sunday school class we discussed non-Christian music. It's a hazy issue for many people, and most of the teenagers in my youth group had difficulty expressing their views. Several of them sounded as though they had no view. We're accustomed to responding to hot issues with answers that have been drilled into our heads by church leaders and parents since we were children. It's challenging for us to probe our minds to come up with our own responses without revealing ignorance and immaturity.

One of the girls, an avid debater, had no problem defining her position. I know better than to believe she has all her beliefs figured out, but she's further along than I am. Instead of interjecting unclear comments now and then, she backed up her statements with convincing illustrations. It was evident that she didn't blindly accept others' beliefs but compared different perspectives.

I want my stand to be as firm as hers. Although not all of her beliefs are firmly established, she is in the process of creating ones free from unwise opinions.

I want to think for myself and form beliefs with prayer, investigation, and time. I don't want to respond to a question by quoting a Bible verse I hardly understand. I want to have the ability to articulate my position with humility and to defend it with confidence.

Teach me how to think for myself and to test the beliefs others share with me. Even if the creeds I come to are the same as theirs, I want to arrive at them through my own efforts. If I struggle with issues, my beliefs will be more powerful and more life-changing.

Do you believe what you do because it's from your soul or because you've been taught that way?

REFLECTIONS: _____

_____

_____

_____

_____

_____

_____

_____

_____

_____

_____

_____

_____

68

The Gift of Love

How precious is Your lovingkindness, O God!
Therefore the children of men put their trust under the shadow
of Your wings.

Psalm 36:7

I sat outside this morning listening to sounds of the far-off train and the playful chirps of nearby birds. I thought of the magnificence of the sunrise and the drops of dew resting on the grass. "I'm a part of this world," I thought. Then I paused and asked myself, "Does God care about and love me like the rest of His creation?"

As I listened to the morning sounds, my delight turned into concern as I pondered that question. I asked, "God, do You love me?"

Sometimes I feel as if You don't. I've been taught that You do and have sung "Jesus Loves Me" so many times one would mock my doubts of its truth. Yet at times it seems You don't think of me as precious and worthy of Your love. Subconsciously I believe I have to earn Your love—that I must work for it and keep working when I get it so I won't lose it. "If I serve God more, He'll be pleased and will acknowledge me," I tell myself. I don't see Your love as a gift.

You do love me, don't You? Even though You're the Ruler of everything, You love me? I feel unworthy of Your love. How can You love someone who messes up all the time?

I long for Your love but don't usually realize how easy

it is to receive. All I have to do is throw away the idea that I must earn it. If I get rid of these false notions of pleasing You in order to receive Your love and working till I drop to maintain Your affection, I will be ready to accept and celebrate Your gift.

God, help me understand the depth of Your devotion to me and delight in my life. I want to feel the power of Your love. Every part of myself cries out for it. I need it, God, and want it as a daughter longs for the love of her daddy.

How can you receive God's gift of love?

REFLECTIONS: _____

_____

_____

_____

_____

_____

_____

_____

_____

_____

_____

_____

69

Perfect Timing

Yet the LORD longs to be gracious to you;
he rises to show you compassion.
For the LORD is a God of justice.
Blessed are all who wait for him!

Isaiah 30:18 NIV

One of my closest friends was unusually quiet today. A tinge of sadness was reflected in her eyes as I spoke with her. I asked if she was upset about something, and she burst into tears.

"You know the guy I really, really like?" she asked.

"Yeah."

"Well, I just found out he's dating another girl," she wept. "I know it's silly to cry when he's not even my boyfriend, but I've never known anyone like him. When I met him two years ago, I knew there was something special about him. I was so excited and hopeful when I saw him last month because he continually stared at me. When we talked his eyes searched mine. I thought maybe God had brought us together. Then I got a letter from one of his friends, telling me he had started going out again with his old girlfriend. I'm so confused."

I told her how sorry I was, but that just because he is dating another girl doesn't mean he's not interested in her.

"It takes time to get to know someone," I responded. "He might be thinking he'd really like to get to know you better, but doesn't know how because you live so far away. Don't think it's the end of the relationship. Remember Captain von Trapp from *The Sound of Music*? He thought he was in love with someone and was about to marry her until Maria came along. Even though it's painful, you may have to wait for God to work in the situation more."

I understand her feelings. Waiting for something fantastic to happen grinds on the emotions. It often seems impossible to say, "God, this is my longing. Please fulfill it in Your time." In Your time may be months or years! However, when I remember the times You caused great things to happen to me after I waited for what seemed like forever, I also remember how amazing and perfect the timing was. You knew what You were doing, even though I didn't.

My heart is encouraged when it realizes the perfection of Your timing. You are an all-knowing God who is aware of and desires what's best for us. Although it seems like an impossible task, putting my trust in You and waiting is what makes my heart strong and secure. I know You will complete what You have begun.

Have you had to wait for something you want, or are you waiting now? What can make it less painful?

REFLECTIONS: _____

_____

_____

_____

_____

_____

_____